D0184317

Project Teams

The Human Factor

Om P Kharbanda
and
Ernest A Stallworthy

MANCHESTER • OXFORD

British Library Cataloguing in Publication Data

Kharbanda, O. P. (Om Prakash)
  Project teams : the human factor.
  1. Management. Team-work
  I. Title   II. Stallworthy, E. A. (Ernest A.)
  658.402

ISBN 0-85554-013-4

LIBRARY

LIMERICK COL
OF ART, C.
& TECHNO.

class no.   658.403 KHA

acc. no: 13777

© NCC BLACKWELL LIMITED, 1990

All rights reserved. No part of this publication may be
reproduced, stored in a retrieval system, or transmitted, in
any form or by any means, without the prior permission of
NCC Blackwell Limited.

First published in 1990 by:
NCC Blackwell Limited, 108 Cowley Road, Oxford OX4 1JF,
England.

Editorial Office, The National Computing Centre Limited,
Oxford Road, Manchester M1 7ED, England.

Typeset in 11pt Palatino by H&H Graphics, Blackburn;
and printed by Hobbs the Printers of Southampton.

ISBN 0-85554-013-4

DEDICATION

Lovingly dedicated to
Ilesha Kharbanda
(born 25 January, 1990 – Ilesha means 'princess')
A precious product of teamwork

Contents

Introduction

A project can be defined as a non-routine, non-repetitive, one-off undertaking, with its own specific time and cost targets. There has been an explosion in the literature on project management in all its aspects.

Success is usually measured in relation to the fulfilment of the pre-set time and cost targets and much of the literature on this subject deals with the techniques used to achieve those targets. As an example, information technology (IT) is playing an ever-increasing role in this area, with a host of computer systems now available to cover various aspects of project management. Nevertheless, we maintain that ultimately it is the human factor in a project, far more than the tools or the techniques, including IT, that determines success. This implies that the composition, training and proper working of the project team is crucial to success.

IT can help considerably in project administration and control, but there is also a negative aspect. With more and more work now being done at home and at other places remote from the office, there is less emphasis on the 'human factor', a factor we consider so vital as to form the subtitle to this present book. Fortunately, and very significantly, current trends in IT are making the worker central to the production process. A high-tech production/manufacturing facility at Lockheed, for example, is based on the need to bring the employee 'back into the manufacturing equation'.

We are convinced that people, rather than materials or

money, are by far the most valuable resource in every walk
of life. Just *one* person, the leader, can make all the difference, but to really achieve anything the leader has to be
supported by an effective team. It is the team, far more than
single individuals or techniques, that successfully trans-
lates the initial concept into a working reality.

Japanese industry provides us with some of the best
working examples of the 'group ethic', or team concept.
Project teams are invariably cross-functional and project
managers integrate, liaise and coordinate the various functions. And irrespective of the team's formal structure, there
is intense, frank and informal communication within the
team and also with the various agencies with whom that
team must work. More and more of the progressive companies everywhere have now started to use the 'project
team' approach quite extensively. It is interesting to see that
this 'team' approach has been extended to their suppliers
and subcontractors as well – with great benefit. A team can
indeed achieve far more than the sum of its members can
ever achieve individually. This is perhaps best exemplified
by a simple proverb, that states that 'one and one *can* be
eleven'.

However, the mere formation of a team is no guarantee of
success. It is very difficult to say what makes a team 'tick',
nor is it easy to establish why one team performs so much
better than another. But in one analogy, with individuals
akin to atoms, the team is rather like a molecule – a discrete
and characteristic entity. Thus a molecule of water is far
more than a mere combination of oxygen and hydrogen
atoms: it is a substance in its own right, with its own very
special qualities and attributes. Similarly, we can consider
the 'chemistry' of teams: the team is very different from the
sum of the constituent individuals. Even this present book,
the result of team effort, is far more than the mere sum of our
individual efforts, were those to be exercised on their own.

Based on the phenomenal success already achieved, the
project team concept is now being extended to most fields of
endeavour, including design, production and marketing.
The 'project team' approach is equally valid in the case of the

mega- or macro-project: by breaking the project down into a number of sub-projects, each can then be tackled on its own. But it is advantageous to have centralised coordination, so that a single agency sees the overall picture and how the various sub-projects are intended to contribute to the broad objective.

A really effective manager today has to do more than just manage. *The effective manager must also be able to lead the team.* We maintain that while leaders can and must manage, a manager cannot necessarily lead as well. This is not just a play on words: the 'managing' function of yesteryear is now yielding to the 'leading' function – tomorrow's role for managers. People would much rather be led than be 'managed', especially since, most unfortunately, this latter suggests being 'manipulated'.

Are leaders born, rather than made? This has been asserted often enough, but we do not accept that view. Managers can be successfully trained to be leaders. The best training is 'on the job', though books and training courses can help. We therefore review in some detail the present situation in relation to management training and development. In assessing the relevance of such training, we see the sort of person that will be required and then study the way in which the essential qualities called for are displayed in action. The future is unknown, but most of the basic problem-solving principles will remain much the same.

Sound leadership is the single most important factor in the success of any project, indeed, of the entire company. An effective leader can help establish tolerance and trust between members of the team and this can indeed achieve wonders. The best engineers, the best suppliers, the best contractors, the best labour force – none of these, not even in combination, can compensate for poor project leadership. This being so, the project manager's contribution to the project is crucial to success. Naturally, therefore, we dwell at length on this aspect.

Fortunately, there is a distinct trend, worldwide, to include business management in the training curricula for existing professions, including finance and engineering. Until recently there has been a fascination, in the educational field, with 'method' rather than an effort being made to *understand* the basic philosophy of management, and more particularly the management of people. We repeat: what is really required in the present uncertain and fiercely competitive business environment is sound leadership. A leader who can not only manage, but also lead the team is the key element today. In fact, teamwork is no accident: it is the by-product of good leadership. This message is coming from many quarters and must be heeded. It is already happening, as our case studies show, and we seek to strongly reinforce this basic message.

Whilst our spread of interests, backgrounds and locations has added to the difficulties of completing *our* particular project, we feel that the book has benefited in scope and flavour. We have both learnt 'the hard way', and we have now brought you some of the lessons we ourselves have learnt over the years.

Part 1

SETTING THE SCENE

1 One Person Makes the Difference

SUMMARY

*We begin by considering the function and role of the team, and establish that a team, to be effective, **must** have a leader. Effective teamwork makes a crucial contribution to the success of a company. When considering the role of the leader, it is essential to distinguish between a leader and a manager: they are not necessarily the same. Whilst some say that leaders are born, rather than made, we are convinced that leadership can be learnt through practical experience; we set out some guidelines in this context. The key to successful leadership is to put people (the employees) first and foremost all the time. We further demonstrate the essential difference between management groups and management teams, using the sports arena as an analogy. The team has a leader, is creative and has well-defined goals. But its success depends upon the **quality** of its leadership.*

INTRODUCTION

This book is about teams in general and project teams in particular. To be really effective, a team *must* have a leader, and that leader is the one person who can make all the difference.

To set the scene let us start by defining the various terms with which we are likely to be involved, by reference to the *Concise Oxford Dictionary*. Here we find that:

- a project is a plan, scheme, or planned undertaking;

- a team is two or more draught animals harnessed together; a set of players forming one side in a game such as cricket or golf; and a set of persons working together.

Hence we also have:

- team-mate, a fellow member of a team;

- team spirit, a willingness to act for a group rather than for one's individual benefit;

- teamwork, working with combined effort, organised cooperation.

What is the primary role or purpose of a team? Why should people act together as a team, rather than work as individuals? Barrett (1987) puts it thus:

> ... teamwork and cooperation ignite and fuel the engines of the individual and the enterprise, and they make a new level of competence possible.

In other words, we work more effectively when we are part of a team. When the primary role of a team is to carry out a project, it is naturally called a project team.

THE PROJECT TEAM

The writing of this book, a carefully planned undertaking, is a project. Starting with the concept, we drew up a draft preface, outlining our objectives, and a table of contents. In this way we outlined the proposed scope of the book. Initially the table of contents was tentative, but its purpose was to convey to prospective publishers the probable content of the book. It was possible that the final result would be substantially different from the initial concept.

The proposal was finally accepted by the publisher and we entered into a contract under the guidance of our literary agent. This project is now complete and in your possession, and you might think that it has been executed by a team of two. But this is not really the case. There were at least three teams working in parallel to ensure the successful completion of this particular project. The literary agent headed a team of experts in that particular field, and there were also several teams working elsewhere to ensure the editing and printing of the book.

In each of such teams, a leader is essential – even in the team of two who wrote the text. The leader usually works through a process of consensus. Issues are taken up with the members of the team, and there may be substantial discussion before a final decision is reached. Having been intimately involved in the decision-making process, the team members should be fully committed to the decisions that are taken, and should proceed to execute their respective tasks with zeal and devotion, seeking to attain the agreed common goal: in our particular example, the publication of a book.

As previously stated, even with a team of two, there must still be a leader: someone who takes the initiative and makes the decisions. In our own particular case, with a history of cooperation extending back over some 15 years and some 15 hardback titles published, there has been a 'leader' in each case, albeit an informal one. A leader is crucial to success. We also believe that we have achieved far more together than either of us would have achieved on our own.

TEAMS CAN WORK WONDERS

There is no doubt that teamwork can work wonders. Of the thousands of articles and books on this subject we thought that we would highlight four, with the following titles (see References for full citations):

1 Entrepreneurship reconsidered – the team as a hero

2 Teamwork responsible for current success

3 Spectacular Teamwork – How to Develop the Leadership Skills for Team Success

4 Teamwork lacking in cockpit

The first article makes the point that teamwork is far more effective in some countries than in the United States. This

LIBRARY
LIMERICK COLLEGE

class no. 658.40$\underline{}$ KHA

acc. no: 13777

has resulted in the early exploitation of some American ideas in those countries, rather than in the United States. Here Reich (1987) suggests that it is the team as a whole who should be honoured as the 'hero', rather than the team leader or any other specific individual. The team leader, whilst often acclaimed as the hero, could have achieved little on his own, and the converse is often equally true. In many cases the team could not have achieved success without effective leadership.

It is for this reason that the US Army has opted to keep teams of soldiers together throughout their entire tour of duty. It is said, in support of this approach, that individuals perform better when they are part of a stable group. They are more reliable. They also take responsibility for the success of their overall operation.

Industrial and commercial companies, both in the United States and elsewhere, are now attaching considerable importance to effective teamwork, and some companies pride themselves on their philosophy and achievements in this regard. Thus a recent advertisement by an American company in the technical press proclaims: 'Bell South is not a bunch of individuals out for themselves . . . we're a team!' Notice the emphasis: a group of individuals is not necessarily a team, but have to be welded together by their leader to operate as an effective unit.

The second article (Purokayastha, 1989), referred to above, discusses the phenomenal success of the Vijay Bank at Bangalore, India. In his first four years as chairman and managing director Sadanand Shetty tripled the bank's deposits and increased the profits a hundredfold. The youngest person ever to be chairman of a nationalised bank, Shetty comments thus:

> I feel I have done what I was expected to do as a chief executive. I built up an efficient team, something this bank needed very badly, and that is primarily responsible for its current success.

A decentralised system of decision making at the top helped to eliminate costly delays, cutting through a maze of complicated processes. It could well have been Shetty's complete dedication to the concept of creating a team spirit that resulted in his rising so rapidly from clerk to chairman. It is no wonder, when he had completed his first four-year term in 1988, that his term of office was extended for another five years.

The first two authors of the book (Blake, Mouton and Allen, 1986) which comes third on the above list are the renowned originators of the managerial grid which now forms a basis for the extensive training of managers. Here teamwork is seen as needing to be understood, developed and refined.

The book describes seven real-life team cultures and explains how teamwork can be inculcated in an organisation. This can be achieved by a series of self-assessment exercises which result in a teamwork grid somewhat similar to the authors' earlier management grid. But the imperative need for an effective leader is paramount. Without an effective leader even a group of outstanding people may just flounder.

The last of the four items noted above – a report in *Times of India*, 23 October 1988 – deals with the disastrous results of a lack of teamwork in a vital industry: aviation. There is *prima facie* evidence that the crash of an Indian Airlines Boeing 737 airplane at Ahmedabad Airport in October 1988 was the result of inefficient cockpit management. There was, it is suggested, a failure of proper teamwork between the commander of the airplane and his co-pilot: the result – disaster.

MANAGER OR LEADER?

We have said that a team must have a *leader*, rather than a *manager*, if it is to operate efficiently. A leader *must* manage, but a manager, whilst still performing his job effectively, may not be able to lead. The difference is crucial to a proper understanding of the subject.

Leadership is very hard to define. To be able to lead well one does not necessarily have to be at the head of the 'pack'.

Often the reverse is true, with the leader not appearing to lead and the 'pack' feeling that they did it all themselves! There is much wisdom in a saying attributed to the Chinese philospher Lao Tzu:

To lead, one must follow.

There are many myths associated with leaders and leadership. Bennis and Nanus (1985) make the point that leadership is a rare skill, but essential at the top of an organisation. They also assert that true leaders are charismatic, ie they have a capacity to inspire devotion and enthusiasm in those they lead. Because of this quality it is said that true leaders are born, rather than made, and that they have the ability to control, direct and drive people towards a desired goal without raising animosity. The successful leader is able:

- to see a picture not yet actualised;
- to see things in the present picture which are not yet there;
- to ensure that the group achieve a common purpose born of *their* desires and activities, rather than *his* purpose.

Bennis and Nanus have highlighted an advertisement in the *Wall Street Journal*. This is an extract:

> ... people don't want to be managed, they want to be led ... you can lead your horse to water, but you can't manage him to drink . . . if you want to manage somebody, manage yourself . . . do that well and you'll be ready to stop managing and start leading others.

Adair (1988a) sets out ten stages in leadership development, with the help of practical examples and case histories. In showing the way to success, he demonstrates the techniques involved in developing a leader and building teamwork at the top of a company, using examples from business, history and the arts. The need for effective leadership is the primary challenge in every field of endeavour.

Fieldler and Chemers (1984), in discussing how to improve leadership effectiveness, present a leadership training method in the form of self-teaching guides. Fieldler and Garcia (1987) present another angle, exploring how and why leaders are effective. It all depends, it seems, on their personality, behaviour and experience. Maddux (1988) demonstrates that a group may not necessarily work together as a team. He cites coal mines that draw upon a common labour pool. There are established regulations and a constant geological structure to deal with, yet worker productivity ranges fourfold, from 58 to 242 tons of coal per employee over a defined period. This vast difference depends entirely on how the management is able to weld its worker into an effective team.

LEADERSHIP – THE FUTURE

Background

We have always felt that experience is the best teacher: to learn from experience it is helpful to consider the past – our own and other people's. The past can well be a pointer for the future, even though the future is largely unpredictable.

Useful observations about the past are provided in the autobiography of Sir Harvey Jones, the British businessman who presided over one of the largest chemical 'empires' in the world, ICI, during the early-1980s. He achieved an amazing turnaround of the company of which he became chairman, transforming a floundering company into a healthy and highly profitable multinational. Towards the end of Sir Harvey's regime, ICI became the first British company to achieve earnings of more than a billion pounds in a single year. How was this achieved?

People Put First and Foremost

Iain Carson, reviewing the autobiography (Jones, 1988), comments thus:

> it is a refreshing breath of air in a subject that needs
> it . . . [he] abhors management by fear. His ideal

organisation is open, blunt, argumentative but *caring about its members much like a successful football team . . . [there is] respect for the individual . . .* if only companies would spend as much time and effort on their people as they do on their capital equipment, they would get both better performance and better results . . . (our italics)

This emphasises that successful leadership is only possible when there is a coherent team or series of teams, and when there is respect for the individual. Recognition of these basic facts transformed the situation at ICI.

Sir Harvey Jones says that no miracle will happen – ie no drastic change will take place – unless *everyone* understands what the goal is and gives of their best to achieve it. This cannot be done by 'buying' people or driving them: they must be *led*.

THE RECIPE FOR LEADERSHIP

How does one develop appropriate leadership qualities? Perhaps the best way is to 'suck it and see'. Take on the role, if you have the opportunity, and learn by hard and perhaps bitter experience. It is rather like learning to swim – you may jump in at the deep end and kick around furiously for mere survival, struggling to keep your head above water. In due course, we hope, the skill comes and you can swim. It can be just the same with the skills of leadership.

We are asserting, you will notice, that the skills of leadership *can* be learnt, and we strongly believe this to be true, despite the suggestion of many that leaders are born, rather than made. Golding (1983) makes this point in a book designed to tell you how to get to the top and stay there. Sir Harvey Jones never suggests that he had some in-born skill or quality: he put his success down entirely to the proper management of people, saying:

Put your people first, above the board of directors, even ahead of the customers, and . . . above the world.

If you put your people first, you win their faith and loyalty, and success will follow. It is a two-way process, the spirit of which is expressed in the saying: 'one hand washes the other'. Surely this is a skill that *can* and *must* be learnt.

Let us assume that you have put our advice into practice, have become an effective leader. This may be after years of painful experience and much trial and error, and you have finally reached the top. You have become, for instance, the chief executive of your company. But how do you stay there? The basic rules are the same as those that brought you there in the first place. You must continue to 'put your people first'. This is not an infallible rule, in that any one of us can meet with misfortune, but the good leader often turns misfortune to advantage.

She has had some luck, people say. But it is really due to her ability to take advantage of circumstances and turn them to advantage. This way we make our own luck. Very few people indeed, when confronted with a crisis or a threat, have the presence of mind and initiative to convert it into an opportunity. But that is one of the attributes of a good leader, particularly one who can stay at the top, having arrived.

It is useful to consider the role of education. Does education help you to become a leader? It seems that education, and more particularly, education in business management, plays a very small part in all this. It seems that the possession of a business degree, such as MBA (Master in Business Administration) may not help and can even hinder, in that it may imbue the owner with a high but unrealistic expectation. Some chief executive officers have such degrees, but seem to be exceptions rather than the rule.

LEADERSHIP IS MUCH MORE THAN MANAGEMENT

Again we can emphasise that managers are not necessarily leaders, that leading is far more difficult than managing. Alan Cane (1988) puts it thus:

Success . . . requires leadership and too often it is

just not there. Management is easy: leadership is
difficult. It requires a breadth of thinking in which
few people are schooled.

What qualities does a chief executive need in order to
survive the challenges of the new and intense global competition in the uncertain and constantly changing business
environment? Cane quotes John Thompson, an international management consultant, who says that the necessary
qualities are, in order of priority:

 −   leadership of a high order;

 −   a clear understanding of the new technologies and
     their opportunities;

 −   the courage to challenge conventional business tech-
     niques.

There seem to be far too few chief executives who have the
right leadership qualities: qualities that will enable them to
steer their 'ship' clear of the economic and business storms.
Thompson sees leadership thus:

Leadership is not about management skills or
about technical competence. It is about paradigms,
mental models of the business. The executive
exhibiting true leadership must constantly re-
create the organisation, challenging the existing
ways – and that takes real courage.

Developments in information systems are also relevant
to the question of leadership. Thompson sees a major trend:
there is emphasis on controlling the channels that exist, ie
the links between supplier and customer. With respect to
existing processing systems, executives often feel frustrated
and even impotent because of their inability to change
existing systems without a massive investment in terms of
hardware, software and people. This seems to be the basic
failing with respect to all present systems: their inflexibility.
The desire to change is at the heart of good leadership, yet
the system inhibits change. Dare the chief executive, acting
as a true leader, throw away all the existing facilities and

start again from scratch? He would like to: it is a leader's innate reaction. To take but one example, surely the existing banking system, which treats valued customers as mere numbers rather than as human beings, should be changed. It seems that the trend is there: banks are now spending vast sums to ensure a customer-based approach as a part of their new and innovative marketing initiative. Surely they are going 'back to basics'!

LESSONS FROM THE SPORTS ARENA

The 'team' concept is, of course, common enough in games and sports of various kinds; hence the sports arena can offer a number of lessons in relation to the successful organisation and leadership of teams. Athletic teams are a good example of interdependence. Each member has a unique function but the team has a common purpose and goal. In the absence of the proper team spirit, teams with high-flying members have been beaten by teams consisting of quite average team members, but who are well coordinated in a team.

To build a team, the team manager has to focus on the largely covert problems, the social and emotional needs of the members of the team. The manager must insist that the group are constantly monitoring and evaluating the process of mutual cooperation. The manager must assess whether team members communicate honestly with one another, their willingness to disagree and express their feelings, their willingness to support one another and hold one another accountable. The manager has to hold the team accountable for solving problems together, whilst adopting a 'guidance' approach. This can be expressed, for instance, by saying: 'I expect you to solve this problem together. If you have any difficulty, I will help you, but you *have* to learn how to solve problems together'. This is indeed the hallmark of the successful team.

The management literature is continually citing the outstanding success achieved by Japanese companies in industry after industry. What is the secret of their success? To explore the question, we can consider the example of one company, Matushita Electric – which it seems has success-fully welded together the best of two cultures, Japanese and European. Successful Western management ploys, organ-isational structure, administrative systems and financial controls have been combined with an Eastern approach to productive interdependence. Instead of the usual compet-itive and potentially disruptive individualism normally encouraged in the West, the Matushita workforce displays a strong cooperative team spirit – a phrase common in relation to sporting events in the West, but not in relation to the operation of companies. What is the lesson? For success it is necessary to build upon the common interests, social and commercial, shared by all.

Comparing Japanese and American management styles, Pascale and Athos (1981) quote Takeo Fujisawa, co-founder of the Honda Motor Company:

> Japanese and American management is 95% the
> same and differs in all important respects.

In terms of the number of techniques, the difference may indeed be only 5 per cent, but qualitatively the difference is most certainly nearer 95 per cent.

Let us illustrate this vital difference by considering the matter of product development by a world leader in print-ers and personal computers. Lorenz (1987) takes the ex-ample of Epson, a company in the Japanese Seiko watch empire. With a decade of explosive growth behind it, Epson used rugby's 'scrum and scramble' approach to develop a new line of printers in less than half the normal time of two years. Already way ahead of all its competitors, Epson is ensuring that it maintains its lead by offering its customers a fast expanding choice of printers at competitive prices.

The 'scrum and scramble' approach is the norm with some other Japanese companies such as Canon, Honda and Sony. It is to be preferred to the sluggish and bureaucratic 'relay race' that is normally used in the West. However, some Western companies, such as Hewlett Packard, have

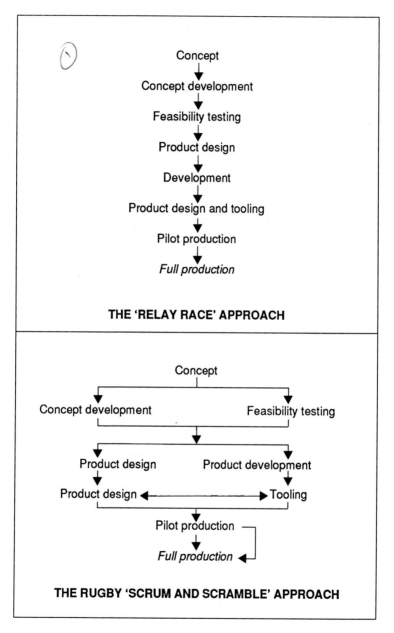

Concept
↓
Concept development
↓
Feasibility testing
↓
Product design
↓
Development
↓
Product design and tooling
↓
Pilot production
↓
Full production

THE 'RELAY RACE' APPROACH

Concept

Concept development   Feasibility testing

Product design   Product development

Product design ← → Tooling

Pilot production

Full production

THE RUGBY 'SCRUM AND SCRAMBLE' APPROACH

Figure 1.1

also adopted this technique. The 'scrum and scramble' approach demands close interaction between team members. Development of the various phases overlap, whereas in the 'relay race' approach they follow one after the other. This overlapping approach to problem resolution places the utmost pressure on the team, which should be handpicked and preferably multi-disciplinary. They work from start to finish on the entire development process, working in tandem rather than step-wise. This type of working seems to come naturally in Japan: more so than anywhere else in the world, and much of their teamwork is informal. We have used the imagery of a 'relay race' and the rugby 'scrum and scramble' because it highlights the difference between a pyramidal organisational structure and a network; or, to put it another way, the difference between the standard bureaucratic process and teamwork. This difference is shown in Figure 1.1.

Continuing the analogy with sport, it is often said that successful corporations have a lot in common with champion football teams. They have patient but active shareholders and lenders, who know when and how much to intervene. If these funders interfere too much, which is very common in private companies, or too little, which is even more common in publicly quoted companies, then the corporation can very easily lose its way. The successful football club has an understanding government, a sympathetic city council and honest referees; they may have star players in all the key positions on the field. Yet all this will come to nothing unless the selectors, the coach, the club managers and the directors also function successfully as an 'off field team', planning strategies, deploying the players and guiding effort. The day of the match-winning superstar, the one-man band, has long gone. In particular, the team needs *leaders*, not cheerleaders. All this is equally true of the company: team effort is today the key to success.

We have been using the terms 'groups' and 'teams' interchangeably, but there is a subtle distinction between the two. Barrett (1987) makes this point, and we can highlight the differences in tabular form (see Table 1.1).

Category	Management Groups	Management Teams
Size	Any number	Nine or less
Chief	Head	Leader
Goal	Aimless	Purposeful and well defined
Driven by	Norms	Clear goal or objective
Structure	Amorphous	Well structured
Manner of operation	Conformist	Creative
Type of organisation	Convergent	Divergent

Table 1.1

The normal management group adds its effort to the whole, whereas with a team there is synergy: the total really is much more effective than would be expected from the sum of the individual efforts.

2 The Role of the Team

SUMMARY

We see that teams are far more prevalent than we might have first thought. Not only do teams work individually, they also work in parallel and cooperate with other teams. We also see that when teams are at work, a great deal depends on the team manager or leader and whether he succeeds in encouraging the team to work together for their common objective.

THE TEAM IN ACTION

The average hospital may be seen as showing many examples of teamwork. In the United Kingdom in the late-1950s the Ministry of Health appointed a work study officer for each of the regional health authorities, with the objective of improving methods and procedures. Over the period 1969 to 1974 a self-financing productivity scheme was instituted, but the need for staff experienced in work measurement and bonus schemes actually led to an increase in the size of the units. The 'team management' concept was introduced in 1974, involving substantial reorganisation. A management services officer was appointed, responsible for computers, work study and statistics. The objective was to control what was in effect a multi-specialist service organisation. Within hospitals there are specialist teams or work groups, responsible for patient care and the necessary support services. Thus, in addition to the medical care, there are ambulance, domestic cleaning, catering, building maintenance and a wide range of other support facilities.

A hospital represents a complex knowledge organisation, and for it to provide a sound and efficient service, diverse specialists have to work together as a team. Such specialists include doctors, nurses, dieticians, pharmacologists, X-ray technicians, laboratory technicians, physical therapists, etc – all working for the benefit of the patient. They carry out their duties as a matter of routine, with only general direction from a doctor. Functionally they report to their respective heads of department, and each professional's work has to be properly synchronised with that of his colleagues. Each individual working for the patient is a responsible professional, and *part of a team*.

The benefits of teamwork are sometimes profiled in advertisements for hospital services. Thus an advertisement for the Hinduja Clinic, a branch of the Hinduja National Hospital and Medical Research Centre in Bombay, is titled: 'Everyone knows the advantage of teamwork – at the Hinduja Clinic, it's applied to health care'. The benefits of the system are enlarged upon in the following terms:

> . . . when, as happens at the Hinduja Clinic, specialists from related fields work together under one roof, as a single team, and meet often to discuss each case, the benefits can be enormous . . . this multi-disciplinary approach means a quicker and more comprehensive diagnosis. For the patient's family doctor, it means a single, comprehensive report, and a clearcut treatment plan for the patient.

The advertisement goes on to say, this is 'teamwork where it does the most good', highlighting the fact that teamwork is essential to good hospital practice.

Another example of hospital teamwork comes from the United Kingdom. Vinten (1989) reports that ten hospitals have formed a consortium to work on their own and each other's problems.

Teams work best if the co-workers are placed together, with emphasis on learning methodologies for finding

answers. There is often too much emphasis on finding the
answer rather than on perfecting the answer-finding methods. In a 'Tribute to Teamwork' the economist Paul Samuelson, of the Massachusetts Institute of Technology, observed:

> There are few pleasures like that of working suc-
> cessfully with one's equal on a hard but tractable
> problem. Research is said to be a lonely business
> . . . How refreshing then to meet with a kindred
> spirit, upon whom one can bounce off conjectures
> and proofs and whose suggestions can be sa-
> voured and digested.

PARALLEL TEAMS

In the typical hospital environment, there are a number of
separate teams whose efforts are coordinated through the
specialist who examines the patient. These teams work in
parallel and have a common objective. This approach can
also be seen working in industry, with teams pulling together in many different ways. For example, a contractor
may be appointed to run a project on behalf of a company.
A project manager is then appointed by the contractor and
is made responsible, within the contractor's organisation,
for every aspect of the project. One contractor says of the
project manager:

> He is responsible for every aspect of the job from
> inception to completion. He is responsible for
> every service required to carry out the work: plan-
> ning, scheduling, costing, designing, engineering,
> purchasing, inspection, shipping, construction and
> commissioning. And he is responsible to you, our
> client. He is your direct contact. And you will
> know him personally. His position calls for wide
> experience, broad knowledge of every group
> within the organisation, the ability to control
> progress and make decisions.

Notice the similarity between this organisation and that of
the hospital. The project manager is analogous to the doctor
whose project is the patient, and is able to call upon a wide

range of specialist groups to perform the various services required, such as design, engineering, purchasing, inspection and construction. Representatives of these various technical groups serve on the project team. However, the company also has to have a parallel project team, since there are certain responsibilities which cannot be delegated to the contractor. This suggests the need for two project teams working in parallel towards a common goal. The organisational arrangement is shown in Figure 2.1. Here it can be seen that the company and the contractor should be mutu-

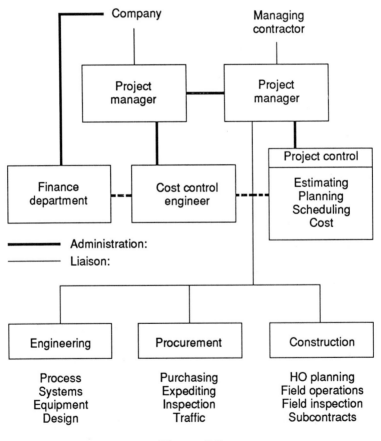

Figure 2.1

ally supportive. This is indeed the way in which the relationship is seen by the contractor, since the layout shown in Figure 2.1 has been copied faithfully from a brochure illustrating the project team as proposed by one such contractor. The heavy rule has been added to the chart as originally prepared and its purpose is explained below.

There is no doubt that this method of working both alongside and in parallel, just like a team of horses 'in harness', is highly successful and can be used in many organisations. How does it work? To quote once again from a brochure issued by a contractor:

> The project control team (see Figure 2.1) under the direction of the project manager sets the control guidelines for the project. On major projects a project control manager heads the project control team. Each supervisor within the engineering, procurement and construction areas involved in the development of the project, controls that which affects his area of work. Thereafter, he is responsible for the execution of the project within the control plans and budget established for his area of work. The project manager, the project control manager and his project control team constantly monitor performance, making adjustments as may be required to plans as they may affect the interfaces between the speciality groups.

It is very clear that this contractor knows the road he has to follow. But the company also has a role to play and this is demonstrated by the 'heavy rule' in Figure 2.1. Two key functions should be exercised by the company within its own organisation. These are the functions performed by the finance department and the cost control engineer – who will have to work alongside the managing contractor's personnel until the project has been completed and accepted. Indeed, they will still be busy when the contractor's team has packed up, left the site and gone off to the next project.

It is interesting to see that the concept of parallel teams is spreading to a number of very different fields. A recent advertisement in the *Daily Telegraph* (11th August 1989) by the electrical distribution companies of the United Kingdom has the headline: 'Successful teams have always produced high flyers'. The text of the advertisement begins:

> Whilst an individual can achieve much on his own, real success comes when the individual is put together with others of like mind. Successful teamwork is about harmonising specialist skills – individual talents working together towards a common goal.

> And that's how it will be when you work with your local Electricity business. Together we can investigate production needs and help you select the right solutions.

So the advertisement goes on, demonstrating the ways in which the electricity supply company can help and support its users. It seeks to demonstrate that the company can be 'a valued member of the production team'. Quite clearly this is yet another context in which teams can work in parallel to their mutual benefit.

DEVELOPING TEAM SKILLS

As we have seen, a team is developed using individuals who have specific skills which are of value in relation to the objectives of the team, whether that be medical care, electricity distribution or completing a major construction project. As the specific examples we have just taken suggest, much if not most of the work in business today is accomplished by teams. This means that proper team building is essential for good management.

Adair (1986) analyses the nature of groups at work and tells us how effective teams are created and developed. The most significant keys to success are:

- to select the right team members;
- to get them to work together;
- to sustain group morale.

Case studies are chosen by Adair to illustrate important principles. It is demonstrated that in many cases there is plenty of scope for improvement in team performance and team leadership.

A team consists of a group of individuals, each with a specific job. Most of these jobs already exist in their own right: they are not created for the benefit of the team and its objectives. The job (or role) of each member of the team should be clearly defined. It is indeed desirable that there be what we can call a position description (see Appendix 1). However, some observers suggest that the position should never be completely defined, since with such rigidity no room is left for creativity. We would suggest that a position description such as that given in Appendix 1 still leaves plenty of room for creative action when that is required. Thus the part to be played by each member of the team is defined.

Each member of the team has to learn to play a part in that team. This is over and above the specific skills that the individual brings to the team, and for which the individual was chosen to be a member. What is more, as you move from team to team, you have to learn your new role in each team – for each team is very different.

What is really under discussion here is what we might call the 'group life'. The individual members, brought together as a group and functioning as a group, have a 'life' of their own and each individual member of the group has to recognise this and contribute towards the objectives of the group. Each individual in the group can both give and receive, and both aspects are equally important. We give according to our own specific talent or skill, but in order to give there must also be a receiver. The receiver is the group as a whole, rather than any specific individual, since the most important thing is the group objective: the reason for which they have all been brought together.

The most challenging task of the group leader is to achieve a balance between the interests of each individual and the interests of the group. This is best done by keeping before all the members of the group their common task. It is the task that they have been given which has drawn the group together and therefore gives them unity. This attitude – a continual reference to the task or goal in view – is the key to success in team building. There is indeed an intimate relationship between the group, its task and each individual member of the group.

The leader should be able to distinguish between the *content* of group discussion and the *process* of group life. It is important to see below the surface and to find out what is actually happening within the group. This understanding will help towards sound decision making.

The leader must keep calm and make it easy for the group members to work interdependently. Whilst the group should aim for a consensus in reaching decisions, this is not always possible and it may be time-consuming. In such circumstances it may be appropriate for the leader, having heard the various views, to make the decision. The ability to reach a consensus depends to a substantial extent on the commitment of the group as shown in Figure 2.2.

If the group is to operate successfully, there must be open communication between all the members of the group. All too often there will be a tendency to form factions within the

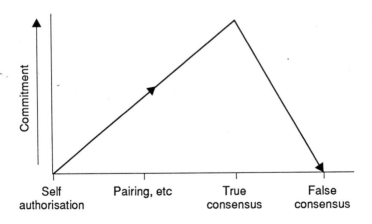

Figure 2.2

group. One must be aware and beware of this, since it means that the team is no longer functioning properly. The team leader must seek to develop teamwork *between* such factions as well as within them. There is also the possibility of a false consensus – where everybody *appears* to agree, but in fact are 'agreeing' not because they accept the soundness of the proposition, but for a variety of 'political' reasons.

THE TEAM IS EVERYWHERE

Ryan (1989) argues that there is no area of human activity where teamwork is not relevant. In stock exchange activities, for example, teamwork has been described as a 'sophisticated management process'.

The main objective of the team leader is to ensure common objectives among the factions and group members. Simon and Farrell (1979) suggest that the aim should be to create:

> a group in which the individuals have a common aim and in which the jobs and skills of each member fit in with those of others, as – to take a very mechanical and static analogy – in a jigsaw puzzle pieces fit together without distortion and together produce some overall pattern.

Teams develop out of the circumstances that prevail. For instance, a person may find that a job is too large for him, and calls in help. That person may then become the team leader. This is the simplest team structure of all, and it is very common. It is one instance of the proliferation of teams in the modern world. Argyle (1972) describes the phenomenon thus:

> Teams are groups of people who cooperate to carry out a joint task. They may be assigned to different work roles, or be allowed to sort them out between themselves and change jobs when they feel like it, for example the crews of ships and aircraft, research teams, maintenance gangs and groups of miners.

ROLES

From this we can see that teams are far more prevalent than perhaps we thought, developing naturally out of circumstances and often lacking formal organisation. Where a relatively simple task is involved, interaction between team members can actually hinder performance. However, it is still possible for the less skilled members of a team to be helped by those members of the team that are more skilled, to their mutual benefit. Where more complicated tasks are involved, teams built up of members with a variety of different skills, able to act on their own, are essential.

It should be recognised that teamwork in industry, for example, has not been uniformly successful. It is all too easy to place people into categories, to label them and then to expect them to fulfil particular roles – and such a facile approach should be avoided. People's roles in a team should be based primarily on their knowledge and skills, not their personality or status. As we have seen, these several roles should fit neatly together, just like the pieces in a jigsaw puzzle, but the puzzle should be as simple as possible. Clear roles and a job specification are essential, but the specification should not be too detailed. Some overlap between jobs is almost inevitable and not undesirable, provided it does not lead to conflict. The successful team will enjoy its work.

Various writers have sought to identify the various team roles. One identifies six:

- Chairman, advancing new ideas;

- Monitor, evaluating those ideas;

- Company worker, translating ideas into practice;

- Team worker, helping and supporting others;

- Resource instigator, sees that what is needed is there;

- Completer, makes sure the work goes out correctly.

It will be appreciated that the above analysis is really focusing on the small company, but as a company grows in size the roles will not change but will be carried out by teams rather than by individuals. Other observers suggest other required roles. The important point is that a team *must* be built up from a number of diverse personalities and that they each have a specific, and different, role to play. We shall be seeing how this works out in practice later.

3 The Road to Achievement

SUMMARY

Compared to a single person, teams can be far more energetic and resourceful. At best they are positive and consistent; their members grow in skills and understanding as team building proceeds; whilst complex problems are solved far more competently than by the single individual. In general, teams have a greater commitment to change than would the team members on their own. However, it has to be recognised that teamwork should not be confined to the lower echelons of a company: teams also have a role to play in senior management. The importance of the leader in holding the team together is demonstrated and emphasised.

THE CHEMISTRY OF TEAMS

How do you go about building teams from scratch? We go into detail in Chapter 9 so for our present purpose let us just say that after assembling the team members, you get them to:

- prepare a statement of their objectives after a discussion that should reach a consensus;

- develop a code of conduct through further discussion that reaches consensus;

- see that the statement of their objectives should state the route they intend to follow to gain their objectives;

- review and discuss their job responsibilities; each
  team member should write a paragraph concerning
  himself for discussion.

The discussion and the striving for consensus outlined
above helps team members to know more about themselves
and about their colleagues. This process has been described
as developing the 'chemistry' of the team. What is meant by
that? A molecule of water is more than the mere combination of hydrogen and oxygen, bound together by strong
forces. Similarly, a team *is* more than the sum of its several
individuals; can *do* more than its constituent members
acting in individual isolation. The power of the group is
seen at its most blatant with a mob. The mob will do violent
things that few of the people in the mob would have
contemplated had they been alone. There is an analogous
chemistry working in relation to the operation of teams,
where, however, the forces at work ought to be guided and
controlled to achieve approved objectives.

Teams develop a sort of synergy which enables them to
accomplish tasks that would otherwise have been thought
to be impossible. What is the secret of the power that
develops within the team? There can be a remarkable po-
tency in integrated effort, which results in force and energy
being focused in the desired direction.

It is factors like these, seen to be associated with teamwork, that have caused many a well-known company to
develop the team approach to management. The Ford Motor
Company, for example, has a highly participative management and employs the teamwork approach. This results in
a working climate that encourages frankness, risk taking
and creativity. Efforts are made to fully involve employees,
thus utilising their enthusiasm and intelligence, whilst giving
them pride and satisfaction in their work. They are all
working together towards a common goal. They have an
agreed mission and a commitment to it. This shared purpose transforms a mere group of people into an effective
team.

DEVELOPING A HIGH-PERFORMANCE TEAM

In order to build and maintain a consistent, high-performance team, an effective leader is required. The quality of a team's performance is very dependent upon its leader.

There should also be proper cooperation between teams engaged in the different steps making up the total operation. To illustrate this point, let us cite the case of a factory making shoes. There are four managers whose activities are fundamental to the effective working of the company: the raw materials buyer, the production planner, the market forecaster and the distribution manager. The efforts of these four should be cooperative: the work of one affects the others. If they don't work together as a team, then their narrow profit margin will disappear. Yet, when we look at the organisation chart for the company, we see these four below the production director, hanging like apples from a tree. There is no indication here that their efforts are interdependent, yet that is what is essential to their success. It may well be happening, but the chart shows them individually responsible to the production director, as though their partners in the business did not exist. Yet they should all be one management team – a team of teams!

There is another aspect related to successful teamwork that needs to be kept in mind. The relationships within the team should be maintained on a friendly basis, with cooperation growing ever closer and more effective. Whilst a clash of ideas is good for teamwork, a clash of personalities within the team is extremely undesirable, to be avoided at all costs. The team faces conflict enough in the marketplace, and can't afford conflict within the team itself.

Teams need supervision to ensure that they attain and maintain a proper standard of performance. Management needs to supervise what is going on, and remove any obstacles that might mar that performance. But the leader often has to deal with the situation as it is: he cannot always have everything he wants. The quality of group interaction for which the leader should be looking is illustrated in Table

3.1, which contrasts individual and group reaction with both normal-team and high-performance-team reaction.

	Individual	Group	Team	High-performance Team
Commonn purpose	lacking	recognised	uses	paramount
Shared responsibility	none	one-way	all-way	all-way
Whole *versus* sum of the parts	less	same	greater	much greater

Table 3.1

POLITICS AND POWER

'Politics' and 'power' are words that have an unfortunate connotation in relation to company organisation. Whilst the words in themselves are neutral, they are often associated with cunning and deceit. Waterman (1987) points out that both politics and power, when misused, are a sure recipe for company stagnation, leading to:

- backbiting;
- no teamwork;
- no shared business values;
- a high degree of diversity.

However, politics and power have a proper place in company organisation. In fact, they are not only legitimate and natural, but essential to the proper management of corporate affairs. At times disagreements can only be resolved by discussion, persuasion and consensus building – and this requires a political approach. At times someone has to exert power and authority: if they don't, progress will be stultified and the company will go downhill.

The ground rules for team development can be summarised:

- the start should be modest;
- aims should be clear;
- development should be self-regulated;
- participants should agree before development proceeds;
- external help should be accepted on occasions;
- learn from your mistakes;
- consult widely and genuinely;
- encourage frank discussion about both principles and practice;
- be realistic about time scales;
- practise what you preach;
- face up to political or organisational problems: do not shelve them.

Persons who are good managers exercise power in excess of their nominal authority and do things outside their defined province. Indeed, in effective companies, this exercise of management responsibility always exceeds the nominal authority. Effective managers do what they see needs to be done, whether or not it is within their job description. A tale is told in this context which is highly instructive. It relates to the time when Ross Perot ruled at General Motors. He saw something that needed doing and he suggested to a manager that he do it. But the manager declined, saying that it was not part of his job. Perot replied bluntly:

'I'll give you a job description: use your head.'

The manager's reply was highly indicative of the sorry state of affairs within GM at the time. He said:

'Can you imagine what chaos we'd have round here if everybody did that?'

Would it have been chaos? General Motors, one of the largest companies in the world, was making a loss, and it was this that caused its management, under the leadership of Roger Smith, then chairman, to revolutionise its approach to company control. The company was seen to be a completely hierarchical and pyramidal structure, with departments operating in isolation, ignorant and indifferent to what was going on elsewhere in the organisation. But this all changed: Roger Smith turned to the Japanese for guidance. Later we shall discuss the role of the Japanese in relation to company management and teamwork. They are masters of the art and we can learn from them.

COOPERATION VERSUS COMPETITION

Winners and losers are the inevitable result of competition – which has erroneously been used in business situations in an endeavour to improve efficiency and performance. Some companies believe that in order to secure the best results they should pit people one against the other, believing that the competitive spirit thus invoked will bring out the best in them.

However, Waterman (1987) points out that relevant research seems to point in exactly the opposite direction. Studies at both Columbia University and the University of Texas have proved conclusively that the best results are secured not through competition, but through cooperation and teamwork. The most productive scientists, it was found, were not moved by competitiveness, but looked for proper work orientation and challenging tasks. In other words, they looked for the challenge in the work they did, *not* in competition with their co-workers.

This research was later extended to cover airline pilots, airline reservation agents, business men and college undergraduates, and in every case the answer was the same. Achievement and competitiveness were inversely related: it was teamwork that achieved success. Why should this be so? One suggestion:

Success often depends on sharing resources efficiently, and this is nearly impossible when people have to work against each other. Cooperation takes advantage of all the skills represented in the group as well as the mysterious process by which that group becomes more than the sum of its parts. By contrast, competition makes people suspicious and hostile towards one another and actively discourages this process . . . competition generally does not promote excellence because trying to do well and trying to beat others are simply two different things.

No wonder that companies noted for the constant renewal of their organisational systems – and consequent success – put a high emphasis on trust and teamwork. Competition erodes both: it's a highly negative force.

Dana, a company in the United States, is outstanding in putting trust above all else. Dana has an enlightened management operating with a unionised workforce, and it remains one of the most successful companies in the trucks and auto parts business. Trust and teamwork are at the heart of operations at Dana. At Dana, employees don't have to earn the trust of their managers and co-workers: it is imputed to them from the very beginning. It is assumed that everyone working for the company does 'what's right for Dana'. Those who do not live up to this concept just do not last long with the company.

Morgan Guaranty is another company where trust reigns, and it is interesting because, being a bank operating across international boundaries, it is so different from Dana. Morgan Guaranty's company culture has trust built into it, right down to the counter clerk, and this is demanded by the very nature of the business. A bank has to have integrity, and this demands trust. Everyone has to work together as a team. This is demonstrated by the company's approach to the profit centre concept, given the rather ill-sounding title 'profit denteritis' on the basis that:

It's not that we don't have profit centers, but [they are] not the be-all and end-all that you see in other institutions. There's a very strong desire to get this bank operating together as a team and pulling together for the long term – doing our best to have every decision we make the best decision for the long haul . . .

Teamwork is the essence of cooperation, and cooperation is invaluable, particularly at times of stress, as when a company is being reorganised. Those working for the company should be involved in the decisions that are being made through a process of consensus.

Again, when faced with a serious problem one should cooperate with others, not strive to do it all on one's own. Others may have met a similar problem and know the answer, thus saving considerable time. It is all very well to be a hero and seek to solve the problem single-handedly, but then there is a high risk of failure. Involving others mitigates against this: the responsibility is immediately shared and thus lessened.

PROJECTS USE PEOPLE

Whilst tools, techniques and facilities are an essential part of any project, the project manager needs, above all, to pay attention to the staff and to help them achieve their goals. Obviously, it will be a great help if the tools and equipment are user-friendly and innovative, and so encourage the team in its work. But all the facilities set up to facilitate the work of a team need to be carefully assessed. Some systems can be cumbersome. If they only police the way in which the team works they can have an adverse effect, so all such matters need careful review and assessment by the project manager.

We must realise that equipment and systems can never be a substitute for people. Information technology, a most rapidly changing area of business services, makes more and more processing power available to users at ever lower prices and smaller sizes. Today, even quite small projects can justify the use of some form of computerised planning and control systems. Unfortunately, the ever-increasing use of such systems seems to mitigate against effective team-work by reducing the human content. Further, it seems that in the matter of project control and progress review, manual recording of data, though tedious, is often the only way to ensure a successful project. Such detailed project analysis not only gives a professional image, but it also teaches many a lesson to the team members, which they can apply when and if they become team leaders themselves. The computer should be used to reduce the administrative load on the team leader, leaving him freer to deal with the management aspects, but it must not be carried to an extreme.

A team needs the range of skills which particular projects demand. In the case of a computer project, for instance, the programmers must be capable of building an effective working relationship with one another and also with the client; the analyst and the designer may well need to convert reluctant users, whilst at the same time giving support and guidance to the programmers. Ultimately, the product must be user-friendly. The type of skills required are both analytical and interpersonal, and the project leader needs to select a team with this in mind.

It is the project leader's responsibility to monitor how the team works, to spot its weaknesses, to encourage team members to mix informally and to get to know one another, to meet members of the team both formally and informally, and to guide the direction of the team. It is of no use for the team leader to select what may well be a perfect team and then sit back. There should be a common commitment: the team should be committed to their leader, and he to them. The leader has to demonstrate this commitment continuously – by action rather than by words.

This is true of almost any type of project. Effective work is done by teams with diverse knowledge and skills, who work together voluntarily for a common purpose. They recognise the dictates of their situation and the requirements of the task: a formal structure is not needed.

Good teamwork involves such aspects as good communications, self-development and the development of others.

This means that the basic communication is sideways, rather than vertical. It is just as important that there be really effective communication *between* the team members as with their superiors.

INVOLVE EVERYONE IN EVERYTHING

This may be difficult to achieve but it is essential. When it *is* accomplished it pays tremendous dividends. People usually feel proud to be involved in matters that are not directly their concern: they find it an honour that their advice is sought and exciting when their advice is brought into effect. Their feeling of pride is translated in positive and productive action: they *cooperate* – fully! Employees at all levels in a company ought to be involved, to some extent, in virtually all the decisions that are reached within the company, and more especially in:

- quality improvement programmes;

- any move towards 100 per cent self-inspection;

- productivity improvement programmes;

- the measuring and monitoring of results;

- budget development;

- budget monitoring;

- the layout of work areas;

- the assessment of new technology;

- the recruiting and hiring of personnel.

All the above items have an impact on everyone within the company, even those not directly involved. The importance of involving everyone in everything lies in the fact that there seems to be no limit to human potential. People often know a lot more about things than we expect, and can make surprisingly substantial contributions when given the opportunity. Involvement results in commitment – and this can bring massive increases in productivity. An essential prerequisite is for management to firmly believe that there is no limit to a person's performance when that individual is properly trained, supported and rewarded.

Despite the rapid strides that have been made in information technology and the increasing use of automation, we remain crucially dependent upon human workers. People are essential to the continuing operation of complex machines. Just a few years ago it was thought that with high-tech information systems, books like the present one, and even libraries as we now have them, would soon be obsolete. This judgement has turned out to be wildly wrong. Many companies have claimed that automation:

- will give a tighter control over labour;
- will reduce staffing levels;
- will rapidly transform industrial activity.

However, the claims have often been excessive; and increasing attention has been paid to the importance of 'people factors'. It is clear, for example, that Japan and Germany:

- have continued to encourage the craft labour tradition;
- have used automation to supplement, not replace, their labour, thus simplifying their work;
- have sought competitive advantage through constant, rapid, refinement and improvement of systems and procedures in which both people and automation are crucial contributing elements.

Where companies *fail* to involve their people, this is the fault of management. Listen, for instance, to Ken Iverson, president of the Nucor Corporation:

> I've heard people say that Nucor is proof that unions *per se* have a negative impact on worker productivity. That's nonsense! That conveniently ignores the vital questions like: What's the quality of direction being given to the workers? Where are the resources the workers need to get the job done efficiently? Where's the opportunity for workers

to contribute ideas about how to do the job better?
The real impediment to producing a higher quality product more efficiently isn't the workers,
union or non-union; it's management.

It seems that many of Nucor's competitors are top heavy,
with a minimum of teamwork. In times of crisis there is
indiscriminate surgery and this hardly leads to the building
of effective teams. In sharp contrast, in a company like
Nucor, the cooperation and teamwork at the top is most
effective, where a management team of three or four can
outperform a host of senior managers in a company without
effective teamwork. At Nucor, communication is quick and
effective, with decisions often made informally.

Management is there to manage, yet management itself
can be *the* problem! We can see from the failures of management suggested by Ken Iverson in the above quotation that
what is lacking is the involvement of everyone in everything. Management fails to seek the cooperation of the
workforce and the end result is disaster. The quality 'king',
W Edwardes Demming, is a little more charitable, maintaining that management is responsible for only 90 per cent of
the problem. But that is near enough to justify one saying
that management can indeed be *the* problem! Labour is not
usually responsible for low productivity, as is the common
misconception. That is almost always the result of poor
management. Management has to recognise and use teams:
that is the way to achieve results. *Everyone should be involved
in everything.*

THE POWER OF INVOLVEMENT

Perhaps the best way to illustrate the merits of everyone
being involved in everything is to take a few examples:
actual case histories can be far more convincing than any
amount of theorising. So, for instance, we can tell the story
of the Buckman's Lab plant in Ghent, Belgium. A 'perfect'
communications system was installed, walkie-talkies being
issued to some eighteen employees. This allowed ware-
house workers to speak to the shipping department and

laboratory supervisors to speak to the production department personnel. But it so happened that the walkie-talkies of two of the workers did not work properly, so that they picked up and heard a lot of chatter that did not really concern them. They listened and got so involved that they volunteered a solution to some of the problems they had heard discussed on the walkie-talkie system. Management was alert, and saw this as an unexpected windfall. As a consequence they downgraded the system, so that *everyone* heard what everyone else was saying. Communication improved tremendously, and do did performance.

Another example comes from a video products company. It was expanding very rapidly and as a result production was failing to meet demand. The several departments involved – such as purchasing, scheduling and shipping – were constantly blaming one another, and the mistakes that were occurring were very expensive. An outside consultant was approached for advice, but to no avail. A full-time coordinator was proposed but this approach failed to provide a solution and turned out to be very expensive. Finally, self-managing teams were established meeting once a week to tackle their problems. There was an immediate and remarkable improvement: the situation quickly improved and profits soared.

Yet another example comes from the coal-mining industry in the United States. One particular mine was running out of coal at the main operating face. To extend the life of the mine a US$24 million project was drawn up by a group of experts, taken from both within the company and from outside. Making a complete break with tradition, a new engineer went underground and chatted with the miners. After gaining their confidence, he was soon offered a very simple and cheap proposal, costing some US$5 million, that would be as effective in extending the mining operations as the earlier elaborate and expensive scheme. With only the half-hearted approval of management a revised scheme was drawn up, further discussed with the miners and finally implemented. It was an outstanding success, achieved at low cost.

If you still have any doubts, consider the case of the Chapparal Steel Company in the United States, which produces products of superb quality without any quality inspectors. How can this be done? Once again it is a question of involvement. The people in the plant are responsible for their own product and its quality. It is said of them: "they act like owners . . . it's really amazing what people can do when you let them". It is said that even the security guards enter data into the computer, and that supervisors do their own firing and hiring and are directly responsible for training their people and for their safety. Every time a new piece of equipment comes into the plant, the foremen and their crews get together and decide how they are going to operate it. Once again we see complete involvement and a total lack of barriers between jobs.

These few examples from among many show that involvement is the key to success. *Yet this is a course which many managements seem curiously reluctant to follow,* despite the fact that it costs them nothing. In none of the cases we have examined were there any additional costs involved in training, or the provision of pay incentives, or increased management support. The personnel directly concerned got involved, and that did the trick. Of course, the real involvement of everyone in everything requires the removal of barriers between functions (remember the walkie-talkie illustration) and the complete abolition of job specialisation.

In one extreme case, following negotiations between labour and management, the number of job categories was reduced from eighty to four! This is the way it should go. Apart from the obvious savings, the psychological benefits of such a change are enormous. Instead of doing the same boring job time and again, workers can have a wide variety of jobs to provide diversion and keep them interested and fully occupied. This can be done, but it involves a fight against a multitude of wrong assumptions concerning the abilities of the average worker.

Part 2

THE NETWORK REPLACES THE HIERARCHY

4 The Pyramid Structure has Failed

SUMMARY

We now examine networking as a system of company management and find that it is far more effective than the traditional pyramidal management structure. Networking requires a certain type of leader or chief executive, but does in fact appeal to people, bringing out the best in them. The effectiveness of (management) networking is demonstrated by the remarkable recovery achieved by the Scandinavian Air System (SAS). There are various theories of management. One assumes that people do not want to work and have to be driven. An alternative theory assumes that people are eager to work, are reasonable, cooperative and capable of self-discipline. Networking demonstrates the soundness of this latter theory.

FAILURE OF THE HIERARCHY

The conventional approach to company management has been to develop a pyramid type of hierarchical structure. This is still used by major organisations such as General Motors and IBM, where power, influence and communication flow down from the top management, its directives and their consequences eventually reaching those at the shop-floor level. Over the years this type of management structure has been both praised and blamed, but the system has persisted.

Naisbitt (1982) suggests that its persistence is largely due to our inertia, coupled with the seeming absence of a better alternative. However, Naisbitt suggests that the hierarchy is being replaced by the networking system, which may eventually become universal.

The hierarchical structure is inherently and necessarily authoritative. This is why it may, perhaps, never be replaced by any other system in, for example, the military services. But in general it seems that people do not really like to be ordered around. People may be forced into doing unwelcome activities because there is the need to hold down a job and make a living, but this type of compulsion has inherent limitations. In such circumstances people rarely work efficiently: the moment they have a choice they are likely to opt for work where they can find job satisfaction and feel valued as people. *People, generally speaking, need to be motivated rather than driven.* This is universally true whatever the size of organisation.

There have been a number of studies that have sought to highlight the weaknesses inherent in the pyramid structure of company organisation, and how these are being overcome. It has been shown that, for example:

- the flow of information is slowed, and this is detrimental to growth;

- the bureaucratic hierarchy is ineffective because of its formal and impersonal nature;

- large centralised institutions have proved too cumbersome: as a result they are being replaced by small decentralised units informally related to one another;

- the ever-increasing use and application of high technology demand close personal interaction in small groups;

- a younger, enlightened and more educated workforce tends to regard the concept of a hierarchy and the pyramid structure as unnatural and unacceptable;

- the Japanese 'miracle' was found to be due to the widespread, almost universal use of small, decentralised work groups, making their own decisions on the spot.

Such findings showed that hierarchies had serious limitations and were, in some cases, largely ineffective. At the workplace it is very natural that people talk to one another, and they exchange information, not only about personal matters, but also about their respective jobs. This led to the informal development of networks within the organisation, a type of contact soon found to be highly effective in terms of getting the job done. Networking, now seen to be a very powerful tool for social action, is increasingly replacing the hierarchical forms of management. It is increasingly acknowledged that hierarchies can lead to much frustration and inertia, damaging staff morale and company performance.

Peters and Austin (1985) demonstrate that the authoritative leader of yesteryear is now rapidly giving place to a very different kind of leader, who has the characteristics of 'a cheerleader, enthusiast, nurturer of champions, hero finder, wanderer, dramatist, coach, facilitator, builder . . .'. A diverse list, but it will be noticed that none of these activities connote ordering people around. On the contrary, their primary function can be said to be that of assisting people to perform their tasks in the most efficient way possible, coaching them when and where required so that they can excel at their job.

This is a most dramatic change in management style, but it has proved highly effective and has made a great difference to the business scene. People are obtaining far more satisfaction from their work, and as a result productivity and efficiency have vastly improved. We have always felt that real-life examples are more convincing than mere words. Therefore we present illustrative case histories later in this chapter.

ROLE OF THE NETWORK

The concept of the network has evolved gradually over the years, some companies taking network initiatives early, others much later. The essence of the network system is that it provides close interaction between people, and this seems to satisfy a basic yearning in human nature. This interaction

– with the sharing of ideas, information and resources – is to everyone's good.

The network concept helps everyone and involves everyone in everything. This involvement is not only at a personal level, but also and more importantly, at the organisational level. The process is quick, brings people into close contact with each other and is highly efficient. There is no time wasted, unlike with the hierarchical system. The quality of life at work improves very considerably and productivity increases markedly.

Let us mention a few of the multitude of network systems that have sprung up in the United States:

-   TRANET (Transnational Network for Appropriate Alternative Technologies). This came into existence in 1976 as a byproduct of the United Nations sponsored HABITAT forum. It serves to link people, projects and resources in the area of their appropriate technology.

-   WARM LINES, a local information in Newton, Massachusetts. This provides information of local interest. For instance, it provides parents with the names of available babysitters.

-   DENVER OPEN NETWORK. This is available to members paying a subscription, and provides access to a computerised file of 500 other people with a variety of different interests. Through this system one inventor found a financier for his new selfcontained water system.

-   NATIONAL WOMEN'S NETWORK. This is based in Washington, DC, and provides information to women on health-related law suits.

These are typical of the thousands of networks that have grown up to meet a need that is becoming ever more demanding. Many of these networks have grown into stable and effective self-sustaining organisations that are doing very useful work in the communities they serve. Some of them are extremely efficient and provide information which otherwise would be very hard to get. The information is provided quickly and is usually accurate. One network, concerned with networking itself, is designed to 'evolve a general understanding of the networking process and the development of an overarching perspective from which to view this vital phenomenon'.

Networks provide a vital and much needed horizontal link, which bureaucracy in general has failed to do. They offer a cross-disciplinary approach to people and issues, whether in social or business life. It has been said that network are like:

> a badly knotted fishnet with a multitude of nodes or cells of varying sizes, each linked to all the others either directly or indirectly . . . whenever people organise themselves to change some aspect of society, a non-bureaucratic but very effective form of organisational structure seems to emerge.

The best thing about networks is that the involved individuals feel themselves to be at the centre of what is going on, and this is precisely why networks are such a success. In a network, people are of the utmost importance: this is crucial to success in the management of companies, and in fact to all successful social relationships. When people see that they are considered to be important, they give of their best, the quality of life improves and productivity increases markedly.

NETWORKS IN THE CORPORATE SCENE

So far we have discussed the character and influence of networks in a very general sense, but we are particularly concerned to see how effective they are within companies. The traditional hierarchical or pyramidal system common in companies provides in essence a vertical link between all the people in the company in terms of administration and control, and communication within the company inevitably follows the same route. Orders are passed down from the top, and they are obeyed by the workforce. There is no discussion or argument as to the merits of the instructions being given. No questions can be asked, and as a result morale is low and productivity poor.

A networking system, using horizontal or lateral communnication, previously non-existent, fills the gaps that exist between people and groups working alongside one another. The network style of management operates informally and even accepts messages from the bottom upwards. At the same time, discipline should be preserved to avoid anarchy.

One of the best known early examples of networking within a large corporate structure was that operated by Intel in the United States, some years ago. Here various effects flowed from networking:

- offices are 'open' and dress informal;

- each worker may have several bosses;

- everyone participates in decision making as equals;

- a high-touch management style pervades the whole organisation;

- purchasing and quality control is a team responsibility, unlike the conventional line staff system, where an individual is in charge;

- even the newest employees can challenge 'superiors';

- executives are stripped of all 'perks', including reserved parking places and separate canteen facilities.

As a result of such changes, introduced via extensive networking within the organisation, many managers report to their peers rather than to their superiors, exchanging information and thus providing a very valuable interaction between one another.

Kanter (1983) makes the point that effective managers

systematically build up a circle of friends both within and outside the company. As a result they have available to them a large network of people constituting a resource which they can turn to as and when the need arises. This is indeed a most effective approach and is the secret of the success of many managers when confronted with a difficult assignment. They can call for help, and they get it. This is true of successful project managers, team leaders and even team members. Effective teams can thus have available to them a valuable network, which constitutes a valuable data bank to which, in an emergency, they can refer for information. How do they manage to cultivate such a wide and valuable circle of acquaintances (friends is perhaps too strong a word)?

It is suggested that they do it by searching for in-house or external expertise that may be lacking in the team. A search amongst those not directly connected with the project may turn up very valuable results. Some of the most significant ideas, for example, have come from teams going out to the marketplace, looking for possible 'gaps' or 'niches' that are just 'crying out' to be filled.

THE MANAGEMENT SHIFT

A remarkable piece of research by Malcolm Trevor (1986), relating to Japanese and European managers in a European setting, has highlighted basic differences of approach. The conclusion reached about British managers, which applies also to American managers, is expressed thus:

> The Japanese expected that managers would not stick to functional boundaries... British managers were over-concerned with a formal chain of command but little concerned with horizontal communication... British managers hoarded information that [the Japanese] managers [in Japanese-owned operations] intended them to share... For British managers, sharing information can be seen as a danger to their career prospects.

With specific relation to Japanese management, these re-
searchers observe:

> jobs are ambiguous, are roughly defined . . . job
> contents change all the time . . . [there are] no
> divisional fences . . . [he] follows company rules
> and procedures very strictly, but his job area is
> very flexible.

These two quotations bring into sharp focus the essential
difference that exists between the old, classical style of
management, using a pyramid structure, and the new style
of management, utilising networking. It should be pointed
out that job flexibility and adherence to rules are not necessarily conflicting or contradictory. To ensure discipline,
rules are essential, but within the framework set by the
rules, it is possible for working areas and responsibilities to
be extremely flexible.

Some companies in the West (notably Du Pont, Hewlett
Packard and Ford) have discovered that there is a substantial payoff in team-level multi-function coordination, but
none of them had gone as far in this field as the Japanese
companies.

A REMARKABLE RECOVERY

The Scandanavian Air System (SAS) was once saddled with
a host of problems, including heavy financial losses. Its
recovery has been credited largely to the transformation of
its management system. Peters (1989) tells us how a conventional pyramidal, hierarchical organisation was changed to
a horizontal cross-functional organisation. This involved:

- a reversal of the conventional pyramid structure;

- middle management serving as a facilitator;

- networking being introduced at all levels.

In the new organisation, the middle manager becomes
the kingpin around which the organisation revolves. He is
the one who can and should 'make things happen', cutting
across the previously sacred functional boundaries. This

drastic change in company organisation was achieved in just two years. SAS lost millions of pounds in 1979–80, but within two years it won the 'Airline of the Year' award by virtue of its high profitability.This occurred at a time when the rest of the airline industry in Europe was making substantial losses.

The chief architect of this reorganisation was Jan Carlzon. His main thrust was to develop a phenomenal improvement in the service offered by the company. The story has been told by him in a Swedish book 'Riv Pyramidernal' (or 'Flatten the Pyramid'), which has now been published in English under the title *Moments of Truth*. But we believe that the Swedish title is far more expressive of what actually happened. Indeed, in our view the new organisational arrangement was such that the pyramid was more than flattened: it was turned upside down!

The management role was seen to be that of supporting the front-line people, the personnel actually flying, maintaining the planes and serving the customer. The role of the middle manager was now that of a facilitator, speeding up the various actions that had to be taken, especially those requiring cooperation between several separate sections or divisions. The middle manager spends most of the time expediting interaction between the concerned departments. The traditional middle-management role of maintenance, inspection, scheduling and hiring is now completely delegated to self-managing teams responsible for these functions. But management must ensure that:

–   workteams are trained and equipped to carry out their allotted function properly;

–   cross-functional bottlenecks are eliminated;

–   they are looking actively for means of operating their unit with increased responsiveness.

The consequence of this policy is that nearly three-quarters of the time of a middle manager is spent on horizontal (or lateral) communication rather than on 'up and down' communication, as earlier. The new organisation, to the extent that there is a pyramidal structure, puts the customer at the top and the board of directors at the bottom (see Figure 4.1). The middle manager now has the power and the authority to say 'yes' and get things done without having to wait for approval from above.

The emphasis is on 'cross-functional' working: the maintenance manager, for example, may well work with his counterpart in baggage handling to speed up things. The aim is primarily to solve problems: to solve them on the spot if possible. He should never pass the problem upward and then wait and see what he gets told. The check-in team at the counters for a particular flight are equipped to answer and handle any query by the passengers. Once again, they do not 'pass the buck' and wait for an answer from on high. The answer should be to hand. It does take time and effort, but the airline has gained enormously in customer satisfaction. According to Carlzon there are 'three moments of truth' in relation to the fleeting contact between the customer and a hitherto impersonal airline. He has declared:

> We don't seek to be one thousand per cent better at any one thing. We seek to be one per cent better at one thousand things.

Figure 4.1

THEORIES X, Y AND Z

In the field of science, theories usually precede practical application, sometimes by many years. In the field of management, however, this process is usually reversed, and practice precedes theory. With management science we are dealing with people, their thinking and their behaviour. People are highly complex in their reactions, and often their behaviour cannot be expressed or predicted mathematically. The management scientist observes human behaviour in a variety of situations and then builds a theory round it.

Theory X is the traditional management theory based upon the hierarchical or pyramid management structure, authoritative and in effect slave-driving. According to Sapre (1976), Theory X rests on three fundamental assumptions:

– man is assumed to be lazy, he dislikes work and avoids it as far as possible, but at the same time he does want security;

– to get man to work, he either needs to be rewarded or alternatively coerced, intimidated and punished – the so-called 'stick and carrot' philosophy of management;

– man has no ambition, does not want to take any initiative and avoids taking responsibility.

This is a grim picture indeed, but it may well reflect the attitudes that prevailed in most countries until a few years ago. With these assumptions there is no trust between the manager and the managed, and hence no cooperation between them. They are in a state of continual antagonism. As a consequence there has to be constant surveillance and control, as in a police state. It should be obvious that no creative work is possible under such conditions: creativity is stifled. The quality of the work life is very poor and as a consequence productivity is low. As a result *everybody* – manager and worker alike – is the poorer.

Sapre (1976) also outlines Theory Y, which was based

upon an entirely different and much more optimistic view of human nature. But he still retained the pyramid structure of management. The basic tenets of Theory Y can be set out as follows:

- work is a natural outlet for human physical and mental energy;

- work is as natural as play or rest; hence everybody normally wants to work;

- people want to develop themselves by learning new things and shouldering responsibility. It gives them a sense of importance and much coveted self-respect;

- people are often unaware of their potentialities but want to explore them, deriving pleasure in the process. People perform best while learning new things and accomplishing difficult tasks;

- people work best under self-discipline and self-direction, hating supervision;

- rewards and incentives help, both those that are extrinsic (promotion, bonus, cash payments, perquisites) and those that are intrinsic (greater freedom, challenging work, happiness at work);

- management must secure the commitment of the people it employs, best achieved using intrinsic incentives in an enlightened fashion;

- management must synchronise the two interdependent needs: the need for self-development for the individual and the need for maximum productive efficiency in the organisation;

- everyone, to a greater or lesser extent, has such qualities as imagination, intelligence, knowledge and sincerity of purpose. This is true of all, not only those in management;

- human resources are far from being fully utilised, since normally full opportunity for self-development is not provided and initiative is often stifled. Management is responsible for the failure to utilise such resources.

This is a long list, but the concept of Theory Y can be seen very clearly. It is *not* soft, slack and weak, as is sometimes suggested. Underlying the theory is a recognition of the fact that the best should be expected of everyone. Everyone is presumed to be reasonable, cooperative and capable of self-discipline. If people have to work mechanically they are stifled. People work best in a creative environment. One can appreciate the difficulties involved in putting Theory Y to work in a hierarchical management structure. So we come to Theory Z, associated with the name of Maslow, the psychologist.

Maslow presented 'a new image of man, a new image of society', but at first was rejected by both publishers and people at large. However, an American company recognised his significance and offered to support him with a fellowship. In Maslow's words:

> The Saga Food Corporation is run in this way – it is a democratising of the boss–subordinate relationship – an effort to appeal to the very highest in human nature, and to set up a work situation in which self-actualisation and personal growth becomes more possible . . .

Maslow postulated a hierarchy of human needs, seen as a pyramid, starting with physiological needs at the base and then going on to safety, love, esteem and finally, at the summit, self-fulfilment (see Figure 4.2). People at the summit were seen by him as falling into two distinct groups: those who were healthy but with little or no self-transcendental experience (eg, Eleanor Roosevelt, Truman and Eisenhower) and those for whom this experience was essential and of paramount importance (eg, Einstein, Aldous Huxley and Schweitzer). Those whom he termed transcenders go beyond Theory Y and seem to live at a higher level, namely Theory Z.

A passage from his work *Eupsychian Management* sums

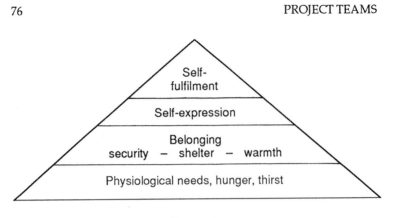

Figure 4.2

up his philosophy. It is set down in the form of advice which an artist gave to his sculptor wife:

> The only way to be an artist is to work, work and work...make a pile of chips...do something with your wood or your stone or your clay and then if it is lost throw it away. This is better than doing nothing...make a pile of chips...act as if you have to earn a living.

A courageous and original thinker, Maslow bridged the gap between Karl Marx's concept of what is good for society, and a yogi's view of what is necessary for personal salvation. Maslow belongs to the human relations school, seeing human feelings as all-important. That is the prime concept behind Theory Z: human relations must be allowed to transcend all other principles.

5 The Network and Company Ownership

SUMMARY

Having seen that the network is replacing the pyramidal structure in company organisation, and assessed the role of training in developing networks, we now consider the relationship between the individuals in a team and their company and its organisation. The network system ensures that individual employees have a much greater sense of participation, and this leads to the concept that they in fact 'own' their company. We assess the way in which this sense of ownership reinforces the contribution which individual members of the team make to team building. This leads to a consideration of the role of communications, especially in the context of emerging protocols and developing standards and the way in which computers can now 'talk' to one another.

WHO OWNS THE COMPANY?

The simple answer is that it is the shareholders who own the company, but usually the shareholders are largely invisible. They do not constitute a coordinated group, controlling the destiny of the company. Who actually determines the fate of a company? Who is it that makes the real sacrifices that ensure a company's progress and prosperity? The unequivocal answer to that question is: the workers. And this suggests that it is the workers who ought to own the company; and of course in a few instances they do.

The Dana Corporation is presented by Peters and Austin (1985) as an outstanding example in this context, since it was

77

the concept of worker ownership that brought about the amazing renewal of this company, once described by its chairman as having the 'rottenest product line ever granted by God to a *Fortune* 500 company'. In a few years the Dana Corporation rose to the number two position, in terms of return on total capital, in the *Fortune* listing. According to Peters and Austin (1985) this was accomplished by translating chairman Ren McPherson's naive but powerful statement – 'turn the company back over to the people who do the work' – into fact.

This was accomplished not so much by buying out the shareholding, as by complete decentralisation of the personnel, legal, purchasing and financial departments. Centralisation looks good on paper, but it never seems to work out in practice. When it come to purchasing, for instance, it is said to give the advantage of volume buying, but that can still be achieved by individual managers, made responsible for their own purchasing, pooling their requirements. They don't need an overriding purchasing department to tell them to do things like that. Having adopted the principle that the real owners of the company were the people who worked there, the Dana Corporation began to proclaim this with a major institutional advertisement that appeared in a number of American journals (such as *Fortune, Forbes* and *Business Week*). This advertisement said:

> Talk back to the boss . . . it's one of Dana's principles of productivity. Bosses don't have all the answers . . . workers know more . . . but all that [knowledge] can't be used unless he's free to talk about it to his boss . . . At Dana bosses listen . . . giving people the freedom to work well to grow and share in the rewards. Our productivity [has] more than doubled in the last 7 years. [We] have also improved our earnings year after year – not bad for a bunch of people who talk back to their bosses.

The company did not stop there. They eliminated a maze of corporate control procedures, such as reports, signing on and off and the like, replacing all that with trust: a trust that treated people as responsible, honest adults. Eventually the majority of the employees (more than 80 per cent) became stockholders. The Dana Corporation is by no means the only major corporation to adopt such policies. IBM is another notable example. Their management is reported as saying: 'We don't need checks and balances. We need trust.' The point is that trust begets trust, and this leads on to success.

TEAMS OF 'OWNERS'

Many Japanese companies have large manufacturing facilities, but their management systems focus on teams and workgroups, each comprising some 10 to 20 people, with high levels of autonomy. This autonomy gives each team a sense of ownership and responsibility for the destiny of their unit and hence of the company.

Although not yet widespread this Japanese concept of management is now on the increase in the United States (and elsewhere). A parallel to the strategy adopted in Japan, but with a difference, can be found in Sweden. Naisbitt (1982) brings us a vision of the corporation of the future as a confederation or network of entrepreneurs, now termed *intra*preneurs, as demonstrated by the Swedish Foresight Group. (Perhaps we should explain that word 'intrapreneur', since it is of relatively recent origin. Intrapreneurship is in effect the setting up of one or more small independent companies *within* the main corporation. The word has yet to find a place in the dictionary, but Pinchot (1985) has written a full-length book about it. The intrapreneur is usually the creator, inventor or innovator of an idea, bringing it to fruition with or without company support.)

The Foresight Group set up a school at Filipstad in Sweden to teach the art of team management to both their employees and corporate managers. The main idea was to encourage creativity in large companies by *actualising* people, so that they bring forward their own ideas and use them: become intrapreneurs. When this is done, everyone profits.

The intrapreneur uses the company's good name, con-
tacts, resources and money – at times, 'on the quiet' – to
bring his ideas to completion, whilst the company retains a
creative person who might otherwise leave the company to
start his own business – that has happened time and again!
The need, therefore, is to restructure the company and
provide flexibility, so that a series of small intrapreneurial
units can operate unhindered. Team spirit is encouraged by
such a working environment and productivity is vastly
improved.

DEVELOPING A SENSE OF OWNERSHIP

Whatever the size of the organisation, the principle of team
building remains the same. The organisation *must* be broken down into a series of small autonomous units or teams.
But unfortunately, people often get in the way: the very
people who can contribute much to teamwork. Managers,
for example, set up hurdles to progress in the form of rules
and regulations, perhaps in an attempt to protect managerial authority. Such efforts are often stupid and irrational,
and at times even malicious. Inappropriate rules can strip
the employee of a sense of ownership and responsibility.

We can consider the case of an aircraft manufacturer with
a turnover of some US$750 million a year. This is a medium-
sized company and it should have had every opportunity
for progress and development, but it was stagnating because of one single problem: quality. Consultants diagnosed the problem as lying with the first-line manufacturing supervisors. It was found that each supervisor was
responsible for some twenty-five to thirty people and up to
US$4 million worth of capital equipment. Yet no supervisor
had the authority to buy even a US$10 can of paint. They
were most certainly not being treated as 'owners'. They had
to obtain the permission of a facilities manager before they
could spend anything. The supervisors were being treated
like children, and this was reflected in their performance.

It seems that demeaning rules are often thought to be
necessary for the proper financial control of educated adults,

such as a first-line manufacturing supervisor. But the supervisor might read into the rule a complete lack of trust. And mistrust begets mistrust. The consultants built up a 4-inch thick report, but the basic principle involved was simple: things had to change if the company were to progress and succeed. The supervisor had to be seen as the leader of a team, and given full responsibility for all that happened within his area of operations, including plant and building maintenance, machine servicing and the like. There are many similar examples: let us quote one more.

The plant manager of the European factory of a large American car manufacturer, employing some 3000 people, was the largest single employer in the town where the plant was located. A local school band requested a donation for new musical instruments costing a few hundred dollars. That request had to go all the way to Detroit for approval, a process taking several weeks. The plant manager was not authorised to say 'yes' on the spot. The consequence? He appeared powerless to his peers, his employees, and the local community – he felt humiliated. Is that good? Where is the sense of common purpose and ownership: the sharing of responsibility? Such silly rules are common enough. The illustrations cited above are in no way unusual.

Top management, when confronted with the issue of 'ownership' and the consequent spreading of responsibility, agree that in principle it is fine, but sometimes say that the unions refuse to cooperate. They also declare that supervisors might feel threatened or overwhelmed by such an increased sense of ownership, with the increased responsibility that it brings. Management, it seems, often bring forward objections because they feel their own status to be threatened.

The solution is to value people as people, to value grownups as grown up and not as children. People must have priority in the company, their feelings recognised and not abused. This is the only sure road to successful company management, but it can be very difficult to put into effect.

TEAM BUILDING

Perhaps we can clarify our ideas by considering a few definitions. Let us first ask ourselves – what is a team? It has been described as a task force or a task group, defined by Chambers 20th Century Dictionary as:

> a group formed by selection from different branches of the armed forces to carry out a specific task: a working part for a civilian purpose.

Teams are composed of people who work together. They are multi-disciplinary, cut across organisational boundaries and are often a 'one-off' arrangement to tackle a specific non-routine and perhaps difficult problem. The terms 'task force', 'team' and 'project team' are largely synonyms, and we have used them in this way. The term *task force* derives from the armed forces, and usually relates to a project of very short duration, perhaps only a few days, but most of the projects we shall be considering are of much longer duration than that.

The prime objective in team building is to develop worker participation, but how is this achieved? It is certain that worker participation, if properly instituted by management, will give personal satisfaction and increase commitment to the company. Such participation is most easily assured through the development of teams and quality circles. Teams are a most effective way to encourage worker participation. Harding (1987) suggests that the team will achieve this via:

- participative decision making;
- creating a feeling of importance and even of belonging;
- creating an effective forum for representation from different departments;
- improved communications;
- creating a sense of corporate identity;
- creating an increased awareness of mutual dependence.

A team's success depends upon its realisation of its goals, a sound knowledge of the techniques involved in operating as a team and the quality of its members. A team is much like a chain, in that it is no stronger, or no better, than its weakest link. The goals to be achieved by the team must of course be consistent with those of the organisation of which it is a part, and its members should have appropriate abilities. Some obvious questions arise when the development of a team is being considered:

- What is to be its composition?
- What is to be the size of the team?
- What are the specific tasks of the team?
- Are its members to be selected, elected or nominated?
- Is the membership of the team to be temporary or permanent?
- Who is to be the leader?

Clearly the answers to these questions will range widely, with the type and the composition of a team varying with its function. To build an effective team it is also necessary to have clear answers to another series of questions:

- What are the limits imposed on the team?
- How much authority and freedom does it have?
- What special skills and/or expertise are required?
- Are any personality problems likely to arise?
- Are team meetings to be open or closed?
- How are the team's decisions to be communicated to management?

There are proven techniques for effective team building, presenting an approach which can be readily adapted to the specific needs of a particular organisation. What is required is a unique and pragmatic synthesis of all the useful ideas that emerge. Organisational development, one of the most exciting managerial concepts of our times, plays an important role. This offers a key to the successful transformation of a company from a pyramidal organisational structure to one built up with networks – so one should learn how to use it. The approach can help good managers become better, and poor or inexperienced managers more competent.

STEPS TO A SUCCESSFUL TEAM

There is a series of stages discernible in the development of a team, and Woodstock (1989) has established some of the more common features. In all, there can be said to be four separate stages, and we set out below their basic characteristics.

Stage 1 – The undeveloped team

This type of team in the most common. It has been formed, but not much thought has been given to the way in which it should operate. The characteristics of the pyramidal organisational structure still prevail, with the result that unusual ideas are not welcomed, the team members are disheartened and personal weaknesses covered up. The team members do their allotted work, often without enthusiasm, and senior management takes all the decisions. This, manifestly, is not real teamwork.

Stage 2 – The experimenting team

Here the team has reached the stage when it is willing to experiment, face the unknown and deal with it. Problems are dealt with openly, and the wider options considered. Hitherto-taboo subjects begin to be discussed, personal issues are raised, feelings come out into the open, and the team members begin to understand one another. Whilst the team is operating openly and effectively, it still lacks the capacity to act in an economic, unified and methodical manner. Some lessons have been learnt, but those lessons have yet to be put to profitable use.

Stage 3 – The consolidating team

This type of team has much more confidence in itself, adopts an open approach and has trust between members. The rules and procedures which prevailed at Stage 1 but which were later rejected, are now being readopted, but as mutually agreed operating rules rather than as managerial edicts. Despite the better relations within the team that were developed in Stage 2, the team learns that some basic rules are crucially important. Decisions are taken by clarifying the purpose of the task before the team, establishing the objectives, collecting the required information, considering the options open to the team, making detailed plans as to what should be done, and finally reviewing the outcome and using that knowledge as a basis for improving future operations. The team is learning as it goes.

Stage 4 – The mature team

The lessons concerning openness learnt during Stage 2, and the systematic approach to problems, developed through Stage 3, have now resulted in a really mature team, wise by experience. Different approaches are adopted to meet different needs and there is a completely flexible approach to problems. Individuals do not seek to defend their position or status, and leadership is decided by the situation that emerges, rather than by protocol. The normal management hierarchy has been completely abandoned, there is individual commitment, and everyone is striving towards the same objective.

ROLE OF COMMUNICATIONS

Communications are important in every walk of life, but this is particularly so in business situations that continuously involve people. Effective communications are basic in all personal relations if misunderstandings are to be avoided, and this is especially important for the team and its operations. Many words can have different meanings to different individuals. 'Planning', for instance, is a much abused and much misunderstood word. It carries different connotations in different companies and much depends upon context. In IBM, for example, a planning system is a means of communication: they don't even talk of the planning process, although the result may well be a plan. Often the main purpose of a formal plan is to remind people of the role of the company. The crux of planning then becomes the *process* of planning, rather than the plan itself. In IBM this process has been formalised; it helps clarify the position on specific items and it also resolves conflicts. Waterman (1987) describes the process thus:

> The staff is explicitly required to take positions on matters that come up via the planning system, and they must do so in writing. They are not allowed the luxury of saying 'maybe'. They must say 'Yes, I agree with that', or 'No, I disagree'. If it's no, they have to fight it out with the line people who are proposing something else, and by dint of superior argument get them to change. If that fails, they and the line people appear before John Akers and the management committee [to argue it out].

Thus planning is being used to develop policy. People become *involved* and *interdependent*: they relate to one another, and this is surely the crux of team building. But a formal process is required to ensure that it happens.

When teams are physically close together, communications are relatively easy, any misunderstandings can be resolved, and clarification of ideas can be obtained and built upon. If they are far apart, the team leader and the team members must take active steps to ensure that there is free, constant and quick communication not only between themselves, but between themselves and other teams with which they may be involved.

There are both formal and informal methods of communication, and some of the informal methods are very effective. One informal method which we believe to be invaluable is what is called 'huddling'. *Huddling – the Informal Way to Management Success* is the unusual title of a book by Merrell (1979) dealing entirely with business communications. The *Concise Oxford Dictionary* defines 'huddle' colloquially as a close or secret conference. Merrell demonstrates that results are produced not by organisations but by people, by a special kind of people – the 'huddlers', who are able to work intimately and informally in small groups. According to him, it is one of the most effective means of communication.

So we are back once again to the team concept, and the importance of close communication within the team. Huddling, of course, is nothing new. It has always been there in the matter of interpersonal relations. It is effective and achieves results. A few minutes of informal conversation with subordinates, peers and superiors, along the corridors of the office or in the washroom, or in the canteen, can be most effective. The practice of this technique, therefore, needs to be encouraged. It is an essential element in good management.

Other informal techniques include the notice board with relevant news items, the weekly lunch together where problems can be exchanged and the occasional telephone call to team members whom you have not seen for some time, to ask how they are getting along. The manager or leader has a more particular responsibility in this area. He needs to be in close contact with *all* the members of the team. One way of achieving this has been given the title MBWA – Manage By Walking About (or Manage By Wandering Around). So many managers rarely leave their offices to see what is happening about them, but they should get out and about.

Whilst we are emphasising the value and importance of personal contact in communication, let us not forget the advantages offered by modern technology, and the way in which it can facilitate communication. This is especially the case when the team members are scattered, as sometimes they have to be. Apart from the usual telephone, the TV conference, the answering machine, the radio paging machine and the car telephone, we can now have computer networks linking all the members of a team, even when they are located in different offices or even on different sites, sometimes across continents.

RESULTS OF RESEARCH

Some research studies have focused on how restricting communication channels affects productivity and the morale of individuals and teams. Five-man groups were studied in circumstances where the communication facilities were varied in a controlled manner. It was found that:

- the most effective group had a 'wheel' pattern, where the four members communicated with only one central person;

- the least effective group was that which operated in a 'circle; however, that type of grouping had the greatest overall morale, since each individual was more involved and hence happier with the group task;

- the intermediate form of grouping, in terms of results, was what can be called the 'chain', or 'Y' structure.

The research established that restriction of communication led to greater efficiency. Whilst this may be true in relation to simple problems, where information must be collated to establish the correct answer, we do not think it is true in relation to the far more complex problems dealt with in manufacturing.

The 'wheel' structure may save the group time in relation to organisation when problem solving, but it is rather inflexible and hence not very efficient when the problems become more complex. In the case of complex problems, a less restricted network, with free communication between all the members of the team, becomes far more efficient. Since that is the more normal situation in industry, a decentralised group structure is to be preferred.

Time and again we have emphasised the crucial role of the group leader or project manager. The style of leadership has also received some attention in research studies. It is often found that the greatest 'productivity' and the highest morale are secured with a 'democratic' leader, who keeps team members fully informed, encourages participative decision making, explains decisions and takes an active but not over-active interest in the group's activities. The 'laissez-faire' leader, who allows the group complete freedom and does not assume an active role, is likely to achieve low productivity. The 'authoritarian' leader, who issues commands but does not otherwise communicate with his group, or give reasons for his decisions, can often succeed in raising productivity, albeit temporarily: however, it is likely that morale in the group is low.

There is no doubt that a participative leader, who communicates freely and frankly, who assumes an active role, who supports team members, who delegates authority and maintains an optimal degree of supervision, is very effective in raising both morale and productivity. These two factors, morale and productivity, are of course directly and positively related.

It is clearly established that the network or team approach is by far the most effective, especially when the team leader or manager adopts a participative role. Further, the more that individual team members develop a sense of 'ownership' in relation to the company, the more effective will their operations be.

6 Information Systems Development

SUMMARY

We now look at the role of the team in relation to information systems development. The best way to develop information systems and the use of the related information technology is by the setting up of a team to carry out a defined task. Problems of setting up and using a team for a specific project are discussed. There are inherent conflicts which have to be overcome. Such teams can be very effective, provided that they are carefully chosen and that their duties and responsibilities are properly defined. This involves a proper evaluation of team performance, with sound team organisation. The team has to be seen as a dynamic, living entity, with a social structure. This means that the proper selection of the members of a team is crucial to its success: guidance on selection is given. Whilst the team leader has a powerful role to play, a dedicated and fully committed team is essential if plans are to be successfully translated into reality.

BASIC PRINCIPLES

We have come a long way from the days when there was serious concern that the advent of computers would dehumanise the workplace, causing considerable unemployment and reducing the roles of surviving employees to those of button pushers. Many such fears have since proved largely unfounded, though there has had to be extensive retraining (and restructuring) to cope with the explosive growth in the use and application of computers. This has been accompanied by a corresponding growth in the amount

91

of related software. Large-scale systems development has become, in just a few years, the rule rather than the exception. The techniques of operation in the workplace have been completely revolutionised.

Such dramatic changes could not have occurred without intensive and extensive team effort. Theories about how such teams operate have developed radically over the years, with present ideas being the result of continuing evolution based on practical trial and error. In the context of Information Technology this began with the use of programming teams in the late 1960s. We now know that there are many factors other than purely technical ones that can and must have an impact. This of course affects the development and content of the team. Yet, despite the tremendous amount of work that has been done in this area, there are numerous problems that make it difficult to develop effective information systems on time and within budget. Fisher (1988) makes the point that much useless data is stored in computer data banks:

> In order to find relevant data nine times as much
> additional irrelevant data will have to be brought
> into the main memory of a computer.

This example suggests that more efficient systems development could lead to more effective functions within the organisation.

In software development there is a great temptation to rush into programming, but this is like laying the bricks of a house without having first drawn up the plans. It seems that when we consider software, many of the normal rules of planning and management guidance just do not apply. Being basically a set of instructions, normally completely hidden from the user, software is a 'hidden technology', most difficult to modify or correct.

For the design of software, there is an optimum size of team. With too few people the project can take longer, since some of the work has to be done sequentially. With more people it can still take longer, since the larger the team, the greater the problems of communication.

COPING WITH THE PROBLEMS

Most of the problems in this area arise from the way in which organisations currently attempt to implement a systems development strategy. For instance, they:

- provide an inadequate level of project management skill and fail to involve management personnel in the development process;

- overemphasise the formal rather than the informal business process – which leads to disagreement amongst team members and managers in the performance of their respective roles;

- lack communication skills;

- fail to establish organisational awareness among their system analysts and program designers.

There is a possible incompatibility between the new technology and the current organisational structure: this should be recognised by management. This incompatibility arises from the fact that the current functional type of organisation does not encourage innovation, yet innovation is an essential element in database technology, since it demands a cross-functional and innovative style of operation. Further, each business has very specific and dynamic needs, whereas the technological products being produced address very general issues and stay static until the next generation of software is produced.

The attempt to resolve problems such as these has led to a team approach and similar techniques designed to encourage team members to understand one another's point of view and so become more open with one another. What is required is an effective methodology which can support and complement the respective efforts of the technician, the management and the ultimate user.

In the process of encouraging a proper team spirit, the domination of the technician has declined over the years. This is very desirable, since the team approach, rather than the individual approach, has proved most promising and is being aggressively explored. Such an approach may well hold the key to the development of more effective systems than has so far been possible.

The more traditional functional approach to systems development has led to a somewhat hostile working environment, where the systems, management and user personnel have really been acting against their overall interests. Rewards and blame are usually showered on the systems development organisation, whilst the traditional reward structure for managers and users has been such as to discourage the development of any team effort amongst them. Further, somewhat contradictory demands seem to be made on the systems professional. The data processing section wishes to constantly update its technology, whereas the user is anxious to employ a safe, proven, albeit obsolete, technology. The position is further complicated by management's insistence on cost reduction as an essential prerequisite to computerisation. This has inevitably led to conflict between systems developers and user personnel.

The initial efforts to develop a team approach did not necessarily bring success, since there was over-simplification. It was assumed, somewhat naively, that the mere creation of a team was sufficient to ensure greater productivity. But increased productivity was not the main or the only objective. What was really required was a proper emphasis on human and organisational issues, with the provision of tools and techniques that would facilitate the full participation of the several team members. The essential elements for success within a team are: select the right people; give them a meaningful role; create the right environment for them to work in.

A team approach can lead to more creative and better solutions to the problems than is offered by the individual approach, even though it may take somewhat longer to reach decisions. But it is very necessary to ensure that each member of the team makes a full and proper contribution. Then, when a decision is reached, its implementation will be much quicker, because of the participation and commitment of the team members.

MAKING THE TEAM EFFECTIVE

The right type of team interaction can ensure success at individual group and intergroup levels. The cooperation of the team members and their individual effectiveness are the essential elements for success, and a most useful by-product of a successful project is the individual satisfaction that it brings. A proper team structure encourages lateral forms of communication and is also amenable to the very desirable vertical linkage between the team and senior management.

Thus an effective team will have an integrating role, a management linking role and a matrix organisational concept. The team approach is essential where the technology and the physical work demanded requires a high interdependence between those involved for success. The social needs of the individuals have also to be met whilst they work together as a group.

Some of the factors that have been found to maximise team performance are:

- the way team meetings are organised and conducted;
- development of an agenda, using chart pads and other techniques to encourage active participation by every team member;
- some formal training of the systems developers in communication skills;
- group decisions, which encourages both the participation and the commitment of individual team members;
- use of an outside consultant to 'catalyse' the team, when personal problems arise.

It is then found that with growing experience the team becomes ever more productive.

EVALUATING TEAM PERFORMANCE

We have repeatedly made the point that the mere creation of a team does not ensure the success of that team. A substantial body of knowledge has been accumulated about team interactions and the necessary skill has now been acquired to analyse and evaluate team behaviour. This knowledge can help to diagnose potential problems before they arise, or reach a critical stage, too late to avoid the collapse of the team. This knowledge has helped build a bridge between the theory on the operation of teams and its application to real-life situations. The major factors that affect team performance fall into five broad categories:

- organisational context;
- physical environment;
- team structure and member selection;
- social structure and interaction;
- task environment and leadership.

It is essential to remember that teams, whether being employed for systems development or for any other purpose, are dynamic entities functioning over a long period of time. Hence no single analysis or evaluation at any point of time can suffice. An initial analysis and evaluation can therefore only be the first step in determining how a particular team is performing. Further, all the above five major factors are not equally important throughout the life of a team. Once one has had experience in collecting relevant data and then analysing it, one can have a clearer understanding of those factors which will most significantly affect team performance at any particular time in its life.

ENVIRONMENTAL FACTORS

A team should be viewed as an organisational, dynamic entity, standing on its own. It is *not* a mere collection of individuals. The group should have a proper structure within the business organisation of which it is a part. Once we see a team as an organisational entity, we can assess its performance at three levels:

- the individual level;
- the team's operation and behaviour;

- the team's relationship with the rest of the organisation.

Galbraith (1977) sees a team as a structural component which has the facility for lateral communication across functional lines. This has particular value when a particular problem or project does not fit into a specific functional area. In introducing this new entity – the systems development team, we must ensure:

- that the team represents the constituency it is designed to serve;

- that it is properly linked to the organisation's management;

- that its objectives are clearly identified and well understood.

Figure 6.1 illustrates this principle in relation to a design department supporting a variety of projects. The design department integrates with the project management function, offering the services of its members on a project basis, with each project calling for different resources. For instance, project 1 does not require any instrumentation, whereas project 5 has no building works: some other contractor has been given that work.

In reviewing and analysing the performance of a team we need to look at questions such as:

- how well is the team performing?

- are there any problems?: if so, how important are they?

- how can we deal effectively with these problems?

Such information must be provided to all the team members, since each one of them should make their own evaluation of the situation. Their evaluation, however, will inevitably be based upon limited data.

Should the team be found to be unrepresentative, it becomes necessary to consider what formal or informal

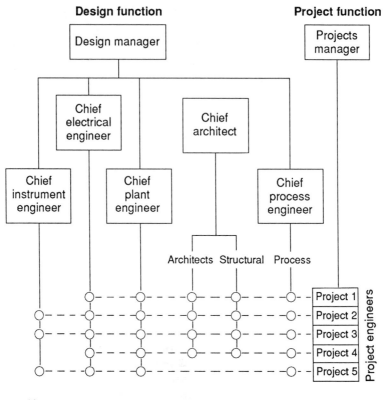

Figure 6.1

adjustments should be made to correct this. Either additional members can be coopted into the team, or there can be part-time liaison with individuals having the requisite specialised knowledge and skill. It is very important to ensure that the team is fully representative, in relation to the task it has been set.

However, team membership relationships can be rather complex, especially in relation to communications and leadership. For instance, if a director or a subordinate supervisor are members of the same team, their participation may not be free and frank. There may well be a tendency for the team to subdivide into groups with specific interests, and the leadership of the team may not be clear. Leadership should be given to the person best qualified in relation to the task in hand, irrespective of his position in the company, or the status of other members of the team.

There can also be misconceptions. A team member may feel negatively about a particular action, but is willing to go along with it if the rest of the team are very positive about it. However, that may well be a misconception by most of the team. An evaluation of the team's progress could well reveal that all the team members share the same misconception and that the team agreed on a particular action because they wrongly thought everyone supported it. At other times some team members may incorrectly believe that their own opinions about a particular action represent the majority view, when in fact that is not the case.

The only sound solution to all such problems is for there to be a frank, honest and free exchange of opinions and feelings amongst the members of the team. They *must* be open and honest with one another at all times. It is then alone that costly and time-wasting misconceptions can be avoided.

The physical environment in which a team works can be a powerful factor in determining not only the way in which it works, but also its effectiveness. This aspect has not received the attention it deserves. Some systems development teams are not even allotted permanent office space where they can meet and work. This is a great mistake: the effectiveness of a team is drastically reduced once its members are physically separated. Indeed, research has demonstrated that the probability of people, working together, communicating with one another diminishes rapidly as the distance between them grows. Figure 6.2 plots the relationship between the probability of people who are working together communicating with one another at least once a week against the distance that separates them. If they

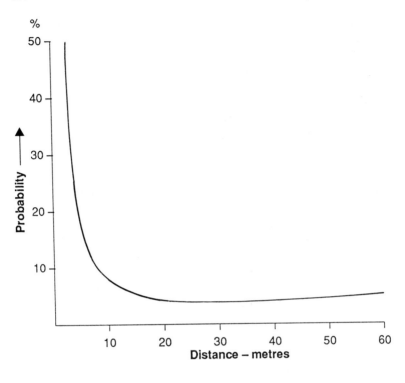

Figure 6.2

work five metres apart, there is only a 25 per cent probability that they will communicate once a week, whilst at only twice that distance, 10 metres, it drops to less than 10 per cent. Beyond 10 metres there is an even steeper drop.

It is certainly desirable to be close for good communication. Those who have had to work in a growing office, where sections have had to be located in separate buildings because of the shortage of space, will have had a practical demonstration of this particular problem and its drastic impact.

For systems development teams, there are three basic dimensions of the physical environment issue: spatial physical barriers (just discussed); communication channel networks; and the environmental cues. It is very clear that the existence or lack of barriers in the work environment will affect the extent and manner of communication, whether that be in formal or informal meetings. It is obviously convenient and normal for people who work together to sit near one another, especially in meetings. Unfortunately, though this at first seems very desirable, it can lead to the formation of cliques within the team, but this in itself would indicate that all the members of the team were not communicating well with one another.

The physical and spatial barriers can involve distance, semi-fixed features such as partitions, and fixed features such as walls. All such barriers hinder people's interaction with one another. They can be designed to increase in-group cohesion, but then the barriers between the team and external groups will be increased. Any conflict between individuals and groups is liable to increase if barriers are removed, although at the same time cooperation and communication within the group will be improved. For these reasons it is very necessary to exercise caution when making environmental changes of whatever nature: they are bound to influence working relationships, sometimes quite drastically and even adversely.

There are several communications alternatives available, ranging from a highly centralised structure, where all communications come through a single member of the team, usually the team leader, to a completely decentralised network. Here the team members communicate directly with one another. It is said that centralised communication is essential for good project management, but we are not satisfied that this is so. It has been found in practice that:

- team members have a higher morale with a decentralised system;

- a decentralised system is more efficient, especially in the solving of complex problems;

- a centralised system can easily become saturated and overloaded.

Environmental cues is the third item on our list. These are

provided when people sit round a table at a meeting. They are affected by the person whom they sit next to, and the frequency of conversation between them. Though one must not attach too much significance to environmental cues, they can provide an early warning that the team is having problems in working together as a cohesive group. In general a systems development project should be provided with a physical environment that will support, rather than hinder, the work that it has to do. This will help to ensure the fullest cooperation and participation between *all* the members of the team involved in the project. The assessment of environmental factors must remain an ongoing exercise, the situation being reviewed periodically. This should ensure that the team is provided with an environment which encourages their working together. Even quite minor factors, such as a coat of fresh paint, a few extra shelves or some pictures on the wall have been found to provide the right environment for better performance.

TEAM STRUCTURE

A systems development team, like any other team, should be seen as a relatively autonomous group. Some of the essential characteristics for autonomy have been identified:

- the group must be entrusted with the whole task, with which it can then identify itself;

- the necessary skills and abilities must be available *within* the team;

- there must be autonomy with regard to work methods, job scheduling and the selection or replacement of team members;

- remuneration should be assessed within the group on the basis of individual performance.

Unfortunately most project teams, when brought together, lack one or more of the above characteristics. But it remains true that complete autonomy is essential if a team is to operate effectively. Of course the autonomy need not go so far as to remove the link between the team and its company management: that should remain. The size of the project team has a powerful influence on its ability to work together. It has been found that teams of from five to seven members are the best: teams of from 12 to 15 members do not perform so well and dissatisfaction with the work develops. Even with a large project, therefore, it is better to keep the basic team size small, and then supplement its efforts by bringing in part-time members possessing the requisite skills and knowledge as and when required. The road to success here is first to create a cohesive team core of say five highly motivated and skilled members. They can then identify such external experts as they may require to further the progress of the work. A variety of disparate backgrounds and technical skills will contribute substantially to the strength of a team. A heterogeneous membership is therefore very desirable.

The selection of the members of a team is perhaps the most important event in its life, yet this has been a somewhat neglected area. The selection of team members should be approached from several different directions simultaneously. There are three major considerations that have to be taken into account:

- the organisational arrangements;
- the objectives of the team;
- the individual.

Team members ought to have the authority to commit the departments from which they have been drawn. They should also have sufficient influence within the organisation to be able to draw upon the resources they need without trouble and of course they must have requisite and adequate knowledge and skills relating to the project.

Other desirable selection criteria include: strong and positive interpersonal skills; a common interest in fulfilling the team's objectives; and a commitment to the team goals. Personal characteristics and work styles also play a vital role in a team's effectiveness. In general, the team members ought to be selected on the basis of their intelligence, knowledge, dependability, social sensitivity and adjustability.

It is also very desirable that the end users of the systems being developed by the team should be invited to participate from the beginning; they should be involved in selecting the team members and organising the team structure. But it remains essential to limit the total strength of the team itself to a small core of full-time members, who have been very carefully selected. Any deficiencies later found in a team when it has been formed can be rectified by some adjustment to its composition, or by providing additional resources on a part-time basis, or by providing the necessary training. Team members should of course be encouraged to help one another in this respect. But as we have repeatedly stressed the mere bringing together of a group of people and describing that group as a 'team' does not necessarily make it an effective team.

It is very necessary that the individual members should see themselves as integral members of the team, each having a vital role to play. This is particularly true when the team is seen as a formal body, brought together to perform a specific task. What is required is a totally informal social structure within the team, with free and totally frank interaction.

The team must see itself as a social entity, each member having a specific role, a certain status and the appropriate amount of power. As a small group, the team will create its own norms, will develop cohesiveness and then operate as an autonomous unit. If there is a high degree of internal conflict, the team is less likely to achieve its goals – but some degree of conflict is inevitable, and perhaps desirable.

Each member of the team has to play a unique and significant role, and will acquire additional status and influence as a member of the team. Working in a team can be very satisfying, but this will only happen when the team is a true social structure, with each individual having a specific role, with its associated status and power. But problems can arise when the team member retains a strong loyalty to the department from which he has been seconded to the team.

This splitting of responsibility may lead to a team member seeing himself as having only a peripheral commitment to the team. This is counter-productive and can even lead to the team member becoming frustrated, and this in its turn will adversely affect the performance and effectiveness of the team. There can also be some discrepancy between the role perceived by a team member and that expected of the member by the other people in the team – due largely to a lack of proper communication.

All this emphasises the prime importance of group cohesiveness. There are five prerequisites for team cohesion:

- the individual member's satisfaction of belonging to a privileged group;

- the degree of closeness and warmth of members towards one another;

- the pride of belonging to a specially selected group;

- confidence that the group can meet a crisis situation;

- the readiness of members to be frank and honest with one another.

Nevertheless, cohesiveness is not sufficient by itself. It is also essential that the team members see that the objectives before the team are consistent with the mission of their company. Further, it is important that the team develops its own formal and informal rules of conduct, ensuring dependability, cooperation and timeliness. There should also be proper criteria for individual praise and commendation within the team, with the appropriate reward for effort. Rewards are powerful motivators and must always have their place.

Today it is recognised that the social structure and interaction within a team needs systematic attention. A careful analysis of these particular factors can help identify those members who are truly participative and have the greatest decision-making influence within the group. This also reveals the extent to which the group is functioning as a team, rather than as a mere group or collection of individuals. For proper team development, it is therefore essential to create an environment that encourages cohesiveness, harmony and unity of purpose. To attain this members should be encouraged to spend sufficient time on group maintenance activities; a facilitator should be identified and assigned to work with the team to achieve these objectives; and there should be periodical team building and training sessions. There should be both internal and external rewards; such as, for instance, a pay structure which involves graduated bonuses at the team level based on the team's achievements. Recognition of the team's performance can still lead to a profound sense of successful achievement by the individual members.

Finally, let us consider the team leader. Desirable characteristics include:

-   the ability to provide direction or structure;

-   the ability to provide support and consideration;

-   substantial influence outside the immediate work group;

-   outstanding task-management skill;

-   ability to identify potential problem areas.

This one person can make all the difference to the implementation of the project, but without a dedicated, committed and fully supportive team little can be achieved. A sound team is crucial to success.

7 Training and Development

SUMMARY

Having looked at the conventional pyramidal company structure, and seen that it has failed and is being replaced by a system of networking that makes use of teams, we now turn to the problem of training and development in relation to teams and team building. We see that the main task is not to change people, nor to motivate them: they are self-motivating. It seems that money (one's salary) is not so important as it used to be, and people are looking first and foremost for a better quality of worklife. Given the right opportunities, people are very ready to assume responsibility, grow into a job they like and thus derive job satisfaction. The emphasis has shifted from the 'loner', following his own career, to the team concept. Now more than ever before people aspire to thrive in a collaborative, team-oriented climate. There are many managements that now realise this and do all they can to cultivate the team spirit within their companies. But a continuous, comprehensive training programme, covering all employees, has to have high priority for success.

LITERATURE UNLIMITED

Training and development for management roles is one of the fastest growing industries. As a consequence we have both a growing body of people claiming competence in the art of training others in management skills, and a vast amount of literature, articles and books – see References.

TRAINING COURSES

To demonstrate how training should be implemented, let us assume that you are the project manager or leader of a team. One of your duties is to see that your team is adequately trained. You hold a unique and very responsible position: the training needs of each member of the team have to be assessed, and opportunity afforded for the appropriate training to take place. There are a host of on-going training programmes offered by various institutions and the value of these needs to be assessed in relation to the training facilities that are available within your own organisation.

We do not expect to have to convince our readers of the value of training. Training, whether on the job or at a training centre will most certainly help the team members to do their job more competently. Adair (1986) lists some of the benefits of training:

- quicker learning as compared with learning on the job;

- better output, improved quality, on-time completion;

- greater motivation, leading to less supervision and better performance;

- the prospect of training attracts better applicants;

- there is more satisfaction at work, hence a lower labour turnover;

- lower costs, both for the company and for its customers.

Everyone can be helped by training, but it is most important to tailor the training programme to the needs of each individual. This takes time and effort, but it is well worthwhile. Then, too, specific training in relation to management may be required. Newer employees in general require more and longer training, partly to compensate for their specific deficiencies, but more importantly, to get them attuned to the company culture and philosophy and to become familiar with the company's products and services. No one can be an expert in every sphere where he may be required to contribute, but with the appropriate academic background and work experience, supplemented by the proper training, one can be better equipped for the work at hand.

To determine the particular skills and knowledge required, it is necessary to assess individual capabilities and shortcomings with specific reference to the job in hand. The best approach is to draw up a job description for each member of the team, preferably in consultation with the individual concerned. Only at this point can a training programme be devised that is appropriate to the situation. Some of the training may well be provided on the job, but it is usually advisable to seek help from outside. Some companies go so far as to have a Human Resources Department or the like, with a training manager, but if that particular facility is not available consideration has to be given to setting up the appropriate training facilities, or ascertaining what is available.

Probably the best way of illustrating the value of training and the way in which it can be accomplished, even in adverse circumstances, is by example. We have described a relevant project in our book *International Construction* (1985). Here we can highlight the training aspect of that project.

The company concerned is the Fife Ethylene Plant, built for Essochem Olefins Inc by The Lummus Company a few years ago.

The plant was built at Mossmorran in Scotland, an area of high employment. Essochem made every effort to employ suitably qualified local residents. This policy demanded an intensive training programme, so Lummus awarded a training contract to the Centre for Industrial Studies at Glenrothes and Buckhaven Technical College. This was for courses for the training of first-line supervisors and was claimed to be the biggest programme of its kind ever introduced into the United Kingdom construction industry. All foremen received four weeks' training prior to having a work crew assigned to them. In addition, every person coming on the site was also required to attend an introductory course at the Prior Lane Centre in Dunfermline, where the purpose and objectives of the project were explained, along with other items of importance, such as safety, site arrangements and working practices. (Making the workforce aware of the objectives of the enterprise is, we believe, an aspect of employee training which is absolutely vital to the success of a project.)

The prospective operators of the plant also needed training. So a temporary building was erected to provide for the training of some 200 plant technicians. There was a formal nine-month programme, after which training continued 'on the job'. All this went forward very successfully, but the training programme had to be so comprehensive because of the shortage of skilled labour at that particular location.

Let us now consider the role of the teacher, and the methods of teaching that are appropriate. Each teacher has an individual style, but the following methods of teaching are the more usual:

- placing the trainee on a project, a real-life exercise;
- business exercises, used for both individual and group training;
- business games;
- the case study method, where a real-life situation is examined on the basis of all the relevant information;
- coaching, involving individual training using carefully planned tasks, with continuous appraisal and counselling;
- group discussion, where a real-life problem is presented to the group and the reaction of the individuals to a group situation is assessed;
- job instruction, involving individual training on the job;
- job rotation, where individuals exchange jobs and so learn aspects of the work of the team outside their own specialisation;

  –   lectures, usually as part of a packaged programme of
       training.

Most of the approaches outlined above can be used either
in-house or at some external institution. In-house programmes have the advantage that they can be tailored
specifically to company needs, and the real-life problems of
the company can be freely discussed. Where the several
members of the team are learning together, this builds
mutual respect and trust, and the project benefits.

DEVELOPING THE TEAM LEADER

Team leaders or project managers have a crucial role. It has
often been demonstrated that the person at the top can make
all the difference (we have dealt with this subject in Chapter
1): the capabilities of the team leader can make or break a
project. And, like all the members of the team, the team
leader also needs training. Let us take another case study to
demonstrate the point.

   Consider a prominent and highly successful international research and development company, here called
RDL International (UK) plc, to preserve their anonymity.
The company specialises in trouble shooting in the motor
industry and their operations include research, the provision of test facilities, with design and engineering departments. The project activity includes various departments
that hold regular review meetings, with coordination at a
senior level. Normal delivery periods had been rather extended, but due to changed market conditions their clients
had begun to insist on much shorter delivery times. Competition had also grown, with two major competitors in Germany and Italy, who had taken a significant share in a
market previously largely an RDL monopoly. How could
they deal with this problem, and regain their market share?
The problems that confronted them within the organisation
included:

  –   how to get the team leaders willing to develop the
       requisite skills, attitudes and behaviour;

  –   how to help them to come to terms with what their job

as team leader demanded, and leave their first love, engineering;

– how to secure genuine commitment without coercion.

RDL wished to regain their earlier position in the market, and this demanded that they so reorganise their activities that deliveries and service met their clients' demands and requirements. Diagnosis led to the conclusion that RDL needed to be more responsive, so that they could quickly mobilise the resources required for any project. This called for a rapid grouping and regrouping of multi-disciplinary project teams tailored to each specific project, backed by the appropriate infrastructure and specialist groups. A director charged with the investigation identified a major obstacle to progress: the existing reward system tended to promote the best technical staff into line management. Further, the prevailing practice devalued people, especially those involved in financial management – this was a highly technical organisation. Line managers were anxious to get involved in technical problems, rather than just 'managing'. This meant that a radical readjustment in their attitudes was required, so that not only managerial but technical and leadership skills were involved at managerial, or 'team leader' level.

RDL's problem is a common one, in that the role of the company and the service it provided to its customers was very different to that required of either its line management or its technical specialists. In effect it was more demanding than either of these on their own. Thus there was a need for people with all-round capabilities, but such people are in very short supply. Hence the urgent need for intensive training of the otherwise promising and well-motivated personnel of the company. This could prove a low-cost but highly effective solution. Once equipped by training, then the project or team leaders can proceed to 'transform' their team members. It was considered vital for RDL to develop the right type of leaders to suit their particular requirements, in relation to the situation prevailing in the organisation. A three-pronged attack on the problem was launched:

1   A research director was charged with RDL's turn-around. He made a presentation to all the team leaders and department heads, setting out his vision for the future, getting them excited about it, and demonstrating the benefits to the employee of the proposed new arrangements.

2   A one-week residential workshop was set up for the team leaders. This was also used for one proposed new team, which was to be charged with a priority project involving some major problems. The workshop was designed to help team leaders develop basic team-leading skills; get an insight into the personal leadership style; help new leaders establish their own leadership practices; agree on success criteria with senior management; outline future action.

3   Two in-house teachers worked closely with consultants throughout the changeover. Having obtained commitment from both sides, the new team went ahead and implemented its agreed programme. This exercise was then repeated with further new teams.

We have not yet heard what degree of success RDL have had, but with such a positive approach one would expect them to regain some of their market share and establish new markets, not only within the EC, but worldwide.

AN EFFECTIVE TEAM

Motivation is an essential prerequisite to effectiveness, not only with the individual but also with the team. To develop motivation in a team is more difficult than with an individual, since each individual in the team has his own specific characteristics and temperament. According to Harrison writing in Lock's *Project Management Handbook* (1987), a group of people can only be formed into an effective team if there is:

- mutual acceptance and trust;
- frank and open communication;
- full cooperation for better and sustained production;

– conflict- and problem-solving through consensus.

When it comes to motivation and team building, our readers should take to heart what Dudley Bennett (1988) says:

> The task is not to change people, [they] are perfectly all right the way they are. The task is not to motivate people, [they] are inherently self-starting. The task is to remove those things that demotivate them, to get out of their way, or . . . to create those kinds of organisational structures that allow workers to get at problems and act in more independent ways so they can develop their skills solving problems related to their own jobs.

This means that opportunity should be given to the workers to act more independently of management, although they should cooperate with their co-workers or team mates. We have described this concept in Chapter 4 as 'networking'. As pointed out there, the pyramidal style of management, based on power, and using fear as the driving force, is seen to be outmoded and is unable to cope with the present-day worker and his problems. Today people are looking for more than just money from their work. They look for opportunity to grow in their jobs and assume responsibility.

Such people thrive in the midst of a collaborative, team-oriented climate. This is where transactional analysis can help. Hidden problems can thereby be brought to the surface and resolved. A study of what is called unit interfacing, that is assessing the boundaries between sensitive areas in the company activities, such as performance appraisal, union negotiations and customer relations, will reduce the problems. The crux of this particular approach is to let the opponent, be it an individual, a task force or a union, become part of the team and thereby see its objectives and make them his own. This will lead to harmonious progress on all fronts.

TRAIN AND RETRAIN

We have discussed the benefits of training, but this should be a fairly continuous on-going process throughout the life of an employee with the company. Peters (1989) makes this point very strongly and quotes Peter Drucker, the well-known management guru: 'Above all [IBM's Thomas] Watson trained, and trained, and trained'. We feel that this must be the foundation of IBM's phenomenal success: with them training is pursued at all levels, all the time.

Cost should never be a constraint when it comes to training. It is a really cost-effective investment. Training at all levels, including individual members of the workforce, should be the top item on the agenda of every company. Today it is only the highly skilled, continuously trained and retrained people who can make a substantial contribution to the progress of a company. The following key points should be remembered when it comes to implementing training programmes:

- train incoming people and retrain them as and when necessary;

- train everybody in problem-solving and quality improvement;

- train a new manager extensively and retrain at every advance up the ladder;

- training must be seen as the vehicle providing strategic thrust in the company;

- training must be line-driven, largely by line people.

The return on the investment in training is fantastic, according to the director of training at Motorola, Bill Wiggenhorn. He says:

> We've documented the savings from the statistical process control methods and problem-solving methods we've trained our people in. We're running a rate of return of 30 times the dollars invested – which is why we've gotten good support from senior management.

Accepting that the human resource is the greatest asset any company has, continuous upgrading of the skills of that resource is a logical and sensible thing to do. Training really

ought to be an obsession with senior management and
nothing should stand in the way of training personnel
regularly and on a routine basis. This is another area where
the Japanese are far ahead of the rest of the world. In Japan,
training is the concern both of the company and of individual managers. As a routine both white-collar and blue-
collar workers go for training in Japan, largely in-house. It
has been found that with Japanese companies the percentage of those who receive more than a week of on-the-job
training is about 30 per cent, whereas in the United States it
is believed to be a mere 5 per cent. Apart from seeking to
train the mind, the Japanese also seek to train the body, and
bring that into a state of well-being, through regular calisthenics, even at the workplace.

DEVELOPING THE TEAM

A group of people working together are not necessarily a
team, but they can be formed into a team with the appropriate training. According to Hill and Somers, writing in the
Project Management Handbook edited by Cleland and King
(1985), there are four distinct stages in team development:
forming, storming, norming and performing. Training in
the form of counselling and coaching is required at each of
these four stages. This training is in fact seen as a five-step
function: educate, sponsor, coach, counsel and confront. In
all this Peters and Austin (1985) see coaching as vital. We
have already discussed the similarity that exists between
work teams and sports teams, so we need not apologise for
quoting the head coach of the Dallas Cowboys (a baseball
team) in this context:

> Perhaps if there has been one failing within our or-
> ganisation over the years, it is that we haven't tried
> to dispel the notion that our success comes out of
> a computer. It doesn't. It comes out of the sweat
> glands of our coaches and players.

The five-step training process outlined above constitutes a
very special and powerful form of guidance, for which there
is no substitute. By far the best coaches are those who set up
a continuous learning process that helps people develop

their skills. Coaching is not a simple matter, but when it is well done it is by far the best contribution that the leader or manager can make to the continuing progress of his company. But coaching is not a single function: it should cover all the five roles we have outlined and in addition the coaching programme has to be tailored to each specific situation. In each of the five roles there are four common hallmarks: timing, tone, consequences and key skills. Ideal coaches vary their approach to suit the person or group they are dealing with and the specific situation in hand, but all these hallmarks have a place.

Consider an example. A most successful cosmetics manufacturer, Mary Kay, has an extravaganza 'seminar' every summer in Dallas, Texas, with countless awards, where the recipients receive much applause. Mary Kay Ash addresses this large gathering of her employees, urging, directing, pushing, advising and seeking to convince almost everyone that each of them can do anything! Is this only show business? We don't think so. We believe it to be educating and coaching, impressing the employees with the company values and beliefs.

IS THERE A PERFECT TEAM?

We must recognise that people are imperfect, but sound coaching can weld a group of imperfect people into a near-perfect team. This point was made by Adair (1986), writing on effective team building, when he said: 'Nobody's perfect, but a team can be'. This is one of the most intriguing aspects of team building, and is responsible for the phenomenal success of management teams in industry. Marks & Spencer, one of the most successful retailers in Britain, and perhaps in the world, offers us a good example. Seeking to establish the proper conditions for effective teamwork, the investment and commitment made by Marks & Spencer in training have been very substantial, and have also been going on for a very long time. But it is suggested that the payoff has been spectacular. Effective teamwork is given the credit by Tse (1985) for the company's enviable record of success in the marketplace.

Usually it is the manager, acting as the coach, who welds a group of people into a 'perfect' team, but we also heard the story of an academician who had not done much throughout his career, but suddenly 'came alive' when put in charge of six youngsters. It is Adair who tells the story:

> John Saunders was 60, five years away from retirement. As an academic he had produced nothing. The head of a newly established Department of Industrial History accepted the suggestion that Saunders should join him. 'Hard luck,' said his present head, 'Saunders is just a deadbeat'. Yet in the lively and enthusiastic company of six younger colleagues, all publishing books and articles, Saunders came alive. In the next ten years he wrote seven books on industrial history.

Where was the fault? Did it lie with his previous head? Perhaps. Obviously there was hidden potential, which lay unused until Saunders was a member of the right team, or perhaps had the right leader. Even very mediocre people can work wonders with the proper counselling and coaching, developing their expectations and increasing their commitment. Training and retraining can really transform the situation, given the right, positive environment.

Part 3

IT TAKES A TEAM
TO DO IT

8 The Basic Theory

SUMMARY

In Chapter 4 we touched briefly on three of the better known management theories, Theories X, Y and Z. We now examine these and some other theories on management, together with research work relating specifically to teamwork, in somewhat greater detail. We then relate these theories to company management to see how theory and practice relate.

THEORIES GALORE

The three most common theories, Theories X, Y and Z, have been mentioned in Chapter 4. To show the key differences between these theories, we set their basic points out in Figure 8.1. Apart from McGregor and Maslow, there are a number of other eminent thinkers who have contributed to this subject, such as Mary Parker Follett and Elton Mayo. It seems that whilst we can give an author to Theories Y and Z, Theory X represents traditional orthodox practice and has no author as such.

Since we have had much to say about the Japanese approach to team building, perhaps we should mention the confusion regarding nomenclature in relation to Japanese management systems and the theories we have been discussing. The Japanese style of management is in fact unique, although it has sometimes been classified as following Theory Z. In our view it is a hybrid, standing somewhere between Theories Y and Z.

Traditional Theory X	McGregor's Theory Y	Maslow's Theory Z
Safety and security	Self-esteem	Self-actualisation
Motivation extrinsic	Motivation intrinsic	Work becomes play
Autocratic	Participative	Impersonal
Interchangeable	Partnership	Saint-sage-pragmatist
Slavelike	Allies	Liberty and humility
God of fear	Loving, kindness	Beyond humanism
Exploitation	Mutual satisfaction	Fusion and merging
Materialistic	Democratic partnership	Spiritual economics
Material science	Humanistic	Cosmic science
Fear	Courage	Beyond both fear and courage

Figure 8.1

FROM INDIVIDUALS TO GROUPS

Certain jobs are best performed by an individual on his own. This is specially true of tasks calling for individual creativity. People like Einstein and Picasso have many goals that they are not prepared to share with others. They operate largely on their own and perform best in this way.

In a normal work situation, however, the only effective way of getting things done is by means of a team. With a team we have the effect of synergy: the team together do far more than they could working as separate individuals. But the team members must have a common outlook, total commitment and a shared goal. But they all remain individuals. How can a group of very different individuals, each with their own likes and dislikes, be welded into a team working together for a common cause? Perhaps two simple models (see Figure 8.2) will help us understand the mech-

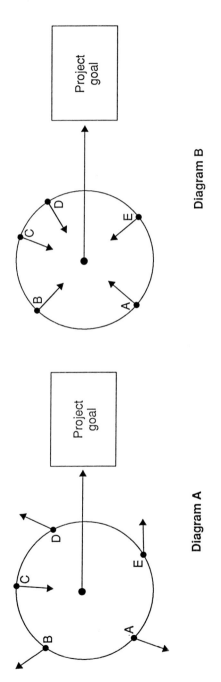

Diagram B

Diagram A

Project goal

Project goal

Figure 8.2

anism involved. Diagram A illustrates the situation when you have, say, five members in a team all working individually. Diagram B illustrates what happens when the same five are working as a team towards a common goal.

How can individuals perform effectively as a group? In team building there are four stages: *forming, storming, norming* and *performing*. The group must perform together and act in a cohesive manner. A leader or a project manager can help, but will take to heart the saying: 'To lead is to serve, nothing more and nothing less'.

The vital question that confronts us at the moment is: how and when does a group of people working together become an effective team? (This is shown in Figure 8.3.) When they are first brought together, the several individuals in a team retain their personal identity, with their likes and dislikes, and often find that they are unable to work together for their common cause. However, with the passage of time the situation stabilises, the status of some of the members of the team becomes established and this process continues until all know their place in the team. This process of stabilisation starts at both ends of the scale at the same time: the senior members and the most junior members rapidly establish their status: it is those in the middle who take some time to sort themselves out. When everyone knows their position and their role in the team, we can say that the team has been formed. How long this process of team formation takes will vary from case to case.

In research experiments, and again in the real-life situation, the leader position stabilises first, but this is not necessarily a result of the desire of the team to have a leader. It is not long, however, before status relationships emerge. In practice, groups seem to stabilise within about a week of continuous working together, or after three to five meetings of a few hours duration. Competition between two groups seems to accelerate this process. Once a group is stabilised it continues to operate without much disruption even during the absence of its leader.

In the course of time, group members come to prefer

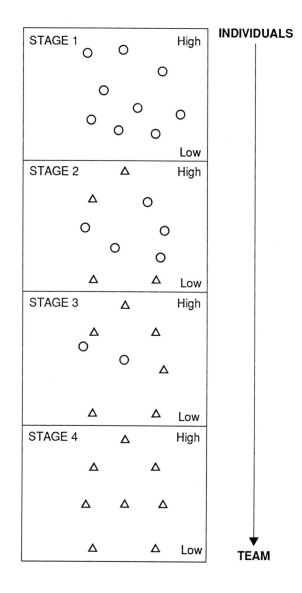

O Team member who has not found a place

△ Team member whose status has been established

Figure 8.3

certain ways of performing particular activities. They may opt for a name, and set up standards for their members' behaviour, both within and outside the group. These norms develop during the process of group formation; that is, during the stabilising period. They are not necessarily the average of the individual behaviour of the several members, but indicate what is considered permissible and acceptable by the group. Such norms are not rigid. They do, however, serve as a measuring scale in assessing the stability of a group. Ways of detecting these norms include:

- observing similarities and regularities in the words and deeds of the members of the group;

- observing correctives offered for certain behaviour and rewards or praise given to others;

- observing the application of the group's norms to a new member of the group.

One of the best indicators of group stability is to observe the degree of consensus amongst the members. A group only becomes effective when it is stabilised.

INTERPERSONAL RELATIONS

As we move, in a management context, from individuals to groups, so the strength increases, but so also do the problems. We can get a negative result if two people are antagonistic to one another. On the other hand, if synergy develops, the power of the group grows. There is strength in numbers, but also weaknesses. Managers need to know and understand the implications of unconscious or covert factors in human interactions, since they have direct relevance to the workplace. Much of a manager's work is dependent on interpersonal relations within the workforce. An understanding of these relationships helps a manager deal with problems.

We have seen that at the heart of most interpersonal problems is poor communications. There are usually a number of unconscious factors arising from interpersonal problems that are at the root of poor performance and discontent at the workplace. These problems are usually reflected in many subtle ways. The employees don't talk of any inability to communicate: they do display loss of motivation, tiredness, or a preoccupation with their own private problems. It is this that needs to be tackled.

The leader-team-member relationship evokes ambivalent feelings. There are both positive and negative reactions to the one in authority. Negative feelings are of course the more difficult to cope with. Whilst they are not normally manifested openly they do mar performance. At times negative emotions are expressed in hostility to another member of the team, rather than to the leader. The problem becomes particularly acute when the leader is too authoritarian. Then a team member with a similar authoritarian attitude becomes the target for open animosity. It will help in such cases if the team leader can rise to the occasion by displaying himself as a scapegoat, the sufferer, whilst all his team members are doing well. This is to put into practice the well-known saying: 'A good king is one whose *subjects* prosper'.

One particular difficulty is that of the 'problem member'. If overactive, this person tends to dominate in group discussion: if underactive, there is little contribution to the work of the team. The services of an overactive member should be retained as valuable to the team. It is, however, necessary to control him in some way: all the other members should have their say, and influence the proceedings. The obvious solution with respect to the underactive member is to get rid of him, but we would not recommend that. The leader should first encourage such a member, drawing him out and searching for latent capabilities.

INTEGRATING A NEW TEAM MEMBER

One way of determining whether or not a team has been stabilised is to observe how it receives a new team member. For the new member to be properly integrated, the leader must play a special role: it will not happen on its own. But the team itself must be functioning properly. If a team is working well, it will be properly managing four areas of effort, thus:

- *The team will have proper goals.* This may seem element-ary, but it is fundamental to the effective operation of the team. The goal, such as making a profit, must be simple and readily understandable; and all members must agree with it. A clearly identifiable and well defined goal is essential.

- *The team members will understand their role.* All members of the team, including the leader, must be clear as to their respective roles. They must all understand who does what, if conflict is to be minimised or avoided.

- *The team will know how to process its work.* The team members have to work together and carry out their jobs. The team leader plays a most important role in this. The work process must cover decision making, and it must be clear who is to participate in this. Good communications are essential to the optimum effect-iveness of the team.

- *There will be proper team relationships.* A good working relationship should exist between all the members of the team. This is crucial. Interpersonal problems *must* be sorted out, and the negative effects of feelings and emotions prevented.

Let us assume the team is effective and has all the four areas of activity mentioned above properly under control. Now a new member is to come into the team. What are the special problems or challenges that will arise when this happens? Careful selection of the new member is the most important aspect. It is essential that the individual goals of the person being selected should be assessed, and these should harmonise with the team goals. But this does not mean that each member should be a clone of the others. Individuality is an asset to the team, and there is substantial advantage in having a 'mix' of members whose knowledge and experience are quite diverse. The new member is most likely to be readily accepted if existing team members are involved in the selection.

The candidate, once selected, is introduced into the work environment. A good group leader or project manager does not *control* others, but his style does set the tone for the group as a whole. The leader must completely accept the new team member, and make this clear to the team. Any hesitation can have serious consequences. It will also help if one or more of the other team members are asked to induct the new member.

UNITY IN DIVERSITY

A team with a range of diverse members is better than one with 'cloned' members. Diversity is more likely to provide the proper mix of talent. But cleverness is not everything. A team of hand-picked and highly intelligent people may perform worse than a team with a much more mixed, average membership. Belbin (1984) cites a management game where, instead of labelling the several teams A, B, C, etc, they were assigned names. One team was called the Apollo team, in memory of the highly motivated and successful lunar mission team. Into this particular team were placed members who had high scores for mental ability; and it was thought that this team was bound to win against the others. But it finished last.

The Apollo team members were, as we would say, 'too clever by half'. Each member was trying to persuade the others to adopt his approach, but no one was prepared to cooperate. These particular individuals were far too individualistic to work together as a team. Whilst trying to reach that elusive cohesion, the immediate, pressing problems were neglected. This exercise has been repeated many times – 25 times over several years – and the Apollo-type team only won three times. This suggests that Apollo-type companies perform worse than other companies, despite their obvious advantages. It seems that:

- they had all the talent but did not know how to use it;
- there was over-emphasis on analysis and counter-analysis;
- they failed to exchange information and coordinate together;

-   there was individual anxiety to stay 'at the top of the
    class'. This inability to be second-in-command led to
    rivalry and a failure to cooperate.

Apollo-type teams *can* produce consistently positive
results, if they themselves are allowed to select their team
members. Then they actually avoid what we might call the
Apollo pitfall, since the nominated leader, himself highly
intelligent, is unlikely to select highly dominant individuals
to share the work. Thus you get a diverse and well-knit team
and have unity in diversity.

Charles Garfield, a member of the team for the Lunar
Module, tells us that the secret of the success of the first
moon landing was the work of thousands of ordinary but
competent people. From project managers to technicians
and secretaries, they suddenly became super achievers.
Why? People had been dreaming for thousands of years of
reaching the moon. Now they were going to do it! The goal
was clear, and all involved were working for success – as a
team.

MORE RESEARCH

Let us consider one concept that deals specifically with the
perception of team members. The objective was to investig-
ate and identify the individual style of a decision support
team and to determine the influence of a combination of
styles on team performance. The research included in-
depth interviews with decision-support team members as
well as key users of the project. These interviews were
highly personal, conducted on a one-to-one basis and using
probing questions to draw out and capture the ideas and the
reactions of those being interviewed. This led to the collection of some vital information in relation to project team
performance.

One objective of the project related to conducting long-
range planning regarding the implementation of an order
entry system, which had earlier been abandoned after two
years' work. This failure was found, on closer study, to be
due to inadequate definition and an inability to interface

with another existing system. The existing hardware was also found to be inadequate for the purpose. However, analysis of the in-depth interviews indicated a narrow perceptual scope at the problem formulation stage by the team, which led to numerous maintenance problems. As a result, valuable information relating to systems problems was never really clearly perceived and evaluated.

As a consequence of this failure, a new project team was designed, taking into account the lessons learnt from the earlier failure. The order entry system designed by the new team proved highly successful. The users found the system to be user friendly, whilst the accompanying documentation was simple and easy to understand. Interviews with this new team confirmed the overall effectiveness of their cooperation.

Each team consisted of ten members, so the percentage of each project team with the designated perceptual styles is shown in Table 8.1.

	Project team 1 %	Project team 2 %
Sensing thinking:	70	40
Intuition thinking:	30	20
Sensing and feeling:	–	20
Intuitive feeling:	–	20

Table 8.1

We see that Team 2, the successful team, is far more balanced than Team 1. It has a far more diverse perception style and it is this, it seems, which has contributed to its success. In-depth interviews with several individuals, including the users of the system, confirmed that critical long-term solutions are more fully developed when all the necessary perceptual styles are represented on the project team. These results have led to the formulation of a theoretical model for the structuring of decision-support teams based on the specific requirements of any given situation. For each requirement there is a dynamic combination of team members that provides the necessary perceptual depth and breadth for the decision-making process.

This research echoes what we have already asserted in far simpler terms: namely that the more diverse the group, the better the team and hence the greater its chance of success. When there is a variety of talent, there is the ability to tackle a host of problems, such as are normally encountered in any project. When a team is made up of a number of very similar individuals, even if they are highly intelligent individuals such as were brought together in the Apollo-type teams, there is far less chance of success.

9 Putting Theory into Practice

SUMMARY

Having set the scene in Chapter 8 by reviewing the basic theory relating to individuals and groups, we now see how those theories work out in practice. We look at the manner in which teams work and their performance in a real-life work situation. We see that whilst the theory seeks to set out the basic foundation for practice, it does not always work out that way: there can be 'many a slip between theory and practice'.

GROUP PERFORMANCE

Experimental studies on group performance largely relate to four major areas: learning, judgment, productivity and problem solving. More often than not more than one of these is involved at any one time. For instance, learning is related to retention, and both are involved in problem solving. Then again, productivity improvement can be the result of creative problem solving. Some of the questions which these experimental studies have sought to answer include:

- how is individual performance affected by the presence of others?

- when is a group more effective than the sum total of its members?

- how can a worker group become more effective?

The level of activity has long been known to increase

133

when people work together. Going back a great many years now, when shoemaking was still a hand process, the case has been cited of a group of shoemakers, where the tapping sounds from the several hammers seems to have served as an additional stimulus for everyone.

Even in word association, vowel cancellation and multiplication tests, it was found that the performance rate of a group was better than when individuals worked alone. Even the learning of lists of nonsense syllables was found to go faster and be easier in the group. In problem solving, too, the group was found to be far more effective than single individuals, perhaps because there was quicker rejection of erroneous solutions as a result of group discussion. This was found to be very much so when the problem had a great variety of solutions. In general a group performs better than the individuals working alone.

The optimum size of the group depends very much on the type of activity being considered. The quality of performance and group productivity are both found to positively correlate with group size under favourable conditions. Really small groups were found to be ineffective whatever the conditions, but otherwise group size appears to have no real effect on the speed with which work is done.

What have become known as the classical Hawthorne experiments related to a group of female workers involved in wiring relays at the US Western Electric plant. The group was placed in a separate room and working conditions were changed with a view to increasing efficiency. It was found that productivity rose: with a change to piece rate working; with increased rest periods; with hot meals and with an earlier quitting time. But on removing these conditions, it was found that the productivity rose even higher. In other words, physical factors were not found to be as important in raising productivity as the cohesiveness of the group and their morale. This had of course developed markedly following upon the segregation of the group and the sense that they were the subject under close observation, and receiving attention.

The Hawthorne experiments confirm the ideas put forward by Herzberg, as reported by Adair (1988), that improvement in working conditions does not necessarily and consistently create a sustained motivational atmosphere. At best they only provide short-term satisfaction, which, it seems, soon evaporates. What really influenced the situation in the Hawthorne experiments was the attention paid to the group. It was this that boosted their morale and so caused productivity to rise. Although these findings have been known for more than forty years, they still seem to be ignored, even by knowledgeable managers. Current 'scientific management' concepts still erroneously maintain that it is the material factors which matter. But this is just not true. They have some significance, of course, but they are the least important of the factors governing sustained group performance. What is far more important to the group is a sense of cohesiveness, purpose and commitment.

TEAM INTERDEPENDENCE

Group cohesiveness and the degree of attention that management pay to the group are vital for better efficiency and productivity. However, over-friendliness amongst the members of the team, resulting in a high degree of sociability and horseplay, can have an adverse effect on productivity. On the other hand, the team's mutual interdependence has a very positive effect.

Technology also plays a vital role in influencing these factors. For instance, the introduction of what is called the 'longwall' method of mining coal in Britain led to a considerable reduction in interdependence between the miners, but surprisingly enough the accident rate increased. It was found that each shift of workers became less aware of other shifts and hence less aware of the extent to which they were dependent upon each other. As a result, shift groups left their work without leaving proper safeguards for the shift that followed them. A solution was found by increasing communication, both formal and informal, between shifts. The management also stressed the importance of interdependence, in relation both to their work and to their goals.

Thus higher technology actually increases the need for interdependence between people, contrary to general expectations.

Research into the role of competition, as compared with cooperation, in relation to productivity and team performance, has had an interesting history. Early studies seemed to show that performance improved with competition, although at times quality suffered. It was assumed that this was due to what we can call upmanship, the desire to excel in a competitive environment. However, later and more sustained studies indicated exactly the reverse. It was shown that cooperation was far better than competition: it brought an all-round improvement in quality, performance and productivity. The reason for this was traced to interdependence, again demonstrated to be a most significant factor in group performance. Of course there are certain working situations when competition can play a positive role, as for instance when people are performing parallel tasks.

In a cooperative work group, the division of labour that ensues is mutually beneficial, assuming that each member of the group is a specialist in his own sphere, yet their mutual interdependence can impose pressures. It is these pressures that result in higher productivity, but they also create tensions. However, the adverse effect of increased tension can be minimised by encouraging greater cohesiveness in the group. This results in increased acceptance of the presence of the other members of the team and a recognition of the fact that they are there to help. However, conditions are seldom clearcut. There can be a range of alternatives, reasons and solutions. This means that one has to seek out the best alternative, a choice that depends upon the situation and the specific goal in view.

CRITICAL SUCCESS FACTORS

Hardaker and Ward (1987) introduce us to IBM's development of what it calls a Critical Success Factor (CSF), based on a quality criterion, within its scheme for process quality management (PQM). The objective is to ensure that every team member knows the direction of the company and what is specifically required of the member for success. PQM was designed to determine customer needs, and at the same time to contribute to IBM's product quality. It starts with a 1–2 day intensive session at which *all* the key managers agree on what is to be done and they each accept their own specific responsibilites. Then the manager assembles a team of some twelve members. All must be present, since PQM not only identifies what is required of each member of the team, but also obtains their personal commitment to what is being proposed. A team is necessary because the project is too large and too complex for one person to handle. This meeting is usually held off the company premises to avoid interruptions. The sequence of steps involved in setting out PQM before the team members is usually:

Understand the mission. Often the members find the mission statement surprising and revealing. The mission statement should be simple, explicit and quantitative.

Specify the goals. It is necessary to get consensus on this, and it is also necessary to detail the critical success factors, both tactical and strategic, that the team will need to recognise if it is to achieve its mission. Each of these factors should be accepted as being necessary and sufficient to enable the team to complete its mission.

Establish what matters most. It is necessary to identify and list what has to be done to meet the CSFs. For instance, do the team need to be more responsive to the market, or to exploit new technologies? Priorities also need to be established.

The follow-through. This is the essence of the CSF/PQM process. In effect, the group are on a never-ending journey to reduce defects to a minimum. The team's decisions must be circulated throughout the organisation. The CSF list itself should be reviewed once a year, or whenever there is a significant change in the team's mission.

There is no doubt that quality improves consistently with such a comprehensive control exercise, and the process should ultimately bring zero defects in the products. However, there are a great many factors that can change a company's mission and its goals: for example, the influence of the government and its regulations, the competition, the need for reorganisation, the development of new technology, and the opening up of new opportunities. But the crucial common factor that has always to be maintained is quality. The team is indispensable when it comes to maintaining quality (chapters in Part 6 are devoted to this aspect).

USING NEGOTIATION

A united team is highly effective in negotiations with others. With a team, more people are witness to what was said, and why. Also, if the negotiations become complex, calling for specialists, they will be there. But it seems that teams are not often used in negotiation. The major reasons are said to be:

- Availability and cost of people;

- There must be tight discipline and each member of the team must have a clearly defined role;

- The organisational rank of the participants can be significant, especially for the other party; yet that has been ignored within the team.

This means that negotiations are often performed by a single individual, sustained by experts when that becomes necessary. However, in certain contexts a team becomes inevitable. This occurs, for instance, when negotiating with some countries, such as Cuba, China, and most other communist countries. Here a team, usually of ten or more, is needed for reasons of morale, even if the extra members are not always required to provide added expertise. There are sharp contrasts in the approach to negotiations in teams from Germany, the USA, Japan, Britain and the Middle East. In Japan the group is all that matters. Negotiations may take three or four times as long as in the West, since everyone in the team must be consulted and a consensus achieved. However, once negotiation is completed the agreement can be quickly implemented since everyone is involved and committed beforehand.

ROLE OF THE LEADER

The most challenging task confronting the leader or manager of a group is to reconcile the interests of the group members and the goal before the group. This is best done by concentrating all the attention and effort of the group on the task they have to perform. It is not the skills of the several members of the group, nor the techniques used, but the correct *attitude* of the team members that will bring success. The attitude towards the task before them is determined by the values which team members place on what they are doing. The way this works is shown in Figure 9.1. The three circles indicate the area of effort of the group and the individual in the group, related to the task that is to be performed. It is the circle overlap that is significant. The

Figure 9.1

group objectives, the individual objectives and the task *must* overlap for success. With an effective team, the individual members of the team are fully involved and motivated, giving their best to the group and to the task before them. It is the task of the leader to ensure that this happens.

A leader, to be really effective, must understand clearly what is going on within the group: its actions and reactions. Through a process of intense observation the leader should get to know and feel not only what the group discusses, but its reasoning processes. It is important to look below the surface and see what is actually going on: *why* people are doing what they are doing. The group's attitude to their leader's exercise of authority influences the way in which they respond to leadership. The group and its leader should be interdependent, and should be able to reach consensus. Whilst a degree of healthy competition within the team can sharpen their skills, this needs to be carefully cultivated and controlled by the leader. It is very easy for subgroups to develop within the groups as a result of such competition, encouraging conflict rather than cooperation. The leader must act as a bridge between the competing factions, ensuring that the common goal is never lost sight of.

THE WORK TEAM CULTURE

Some of the new participative management approaches – such as job enrichment, quality circles and self-managing work teams – are now gaining widespread popularity. They all have the common goal of increasing employee involvement and commitment. The work team is but one aspect of participative management, but it has received widespread acceptance, largely because it is the basis of Japanese management systems. Indeed, Lawler (1986) sees it as the answer to the Japanese challenge. He demonstrates, by example, the way in which companies in the United States have responded. For instance:

- General Motors use teams for motorcar assembly and motorcar design and development. Their Saturn car was developed by teams.

- The Butler Manufacturing Company uses work teams to assemble grain elevators.

- The General Electric Company was one of the pioneers with work teams in the United States. During the 1960s they formed over a hundred teams, although some of these disappeared after a while.

- Shell Chemical, at their plant in Sarnia, Ontario, set a work team responsible for the running of the entire plant complex.

- At the Cummins Engine Plant, Jamestown, New York, one work team is responsible for machining and another for work on the entire engine.

These are typical examples of a developing process in relation to work teams. It is not confined to the United States. The same concept has been gaining momentum in the United Kingdom. For example, in the British coal industry the workers spontaneously created their own work teams at the coal face, with team members helping one another out and even at times exchanging jobs. This has brought higher productivity together with job satisfaction and was far more effective than the traditional system it replaced, where workers had their own specific trades which they followed. In Europe the same movement can be seen. Volvo is an outstanding example: their car manufacturing plant at Kalmar, Sweden, is built around work teams, rather than the more usual assembly line production. One work team is responsible for putting in the complete electrical system, another for fitting all the upholstery, and so on.

THE WORK TEAM IN OPERATION

How do these work teams cooperate together? As one would expect, the way in which they work will vary from case to case. It all depends upon the history of the particular company when they are established. Each company will have its own working environment, and the work teams are set up to deal with an existing production requirement. There are not many factories as yet where the work team concept has been brought in right at the beginning. Lawler

(1986), however, draws our attention to a number of factors that are common to all such work team arrangements:

Membership. To be fully effective *everyone* working in the relevant area must be included in the work team. This includes maintenance teams and even the cleaners. This means that very often the concept has to be introduced very slowly, and first of all in areas where an interest is being displayed.

Work area coverage. Each team must be *in charge* of an entire product or service, so that there is clear input and output, ie the responsibilities of the work team can be very simply and precisely defined. The case of Volvo, cited above, is illustrative of this approach, eg the *complete* electrical system on a car is assigned to one work team.

Training. What we can call cross training is essential, ie there must be constant work rotation between team members so that they are all completely familiar with each other's work. This also adds to the interest of the work: it becomes far less monotonous.

Meetings. There should be frequent meetings of all the members of the team. These meetings should be scheduled to be at least weekly, and more often if the necessity arises.

Supervision. A leader is either appointed, or voted in by the members themselves. The leader will have to be extremely active initially, with a diminishing role as the team gains experience in working together. The leader should aim to become a facilitator and communicator, linking the team with management and other teams.

Decision making. All the members of the team must be involved in decision making, so that they have a sense of belonging and a commitment towards the accomplishment of what has been agreed.

Setting up the team. Typically a team will be installed in an existing facility and first of all on an experimental basis. It can take from two to three years for a work team to become fully effective, and senior management must recognise this and have patience.

Team size. The optimum number of team members seems to be between seven and fifteen. Larger groups tend to have less cohesion, and hence to have less identity of purpose.

THE IMPACT OF CRISIS

It seems that more often than not teams are introduced into a company at a time of crisis. The company runs into trouble, and the setting up of teams is seen as the way out of trouble. Waterman (1987) points out that the Chinese word for crisis also means opportunity. We can see that every crisis offers an opportunity to be exploited. A heart attack can serve as a much-needed warning and be a sure way of putting an overweight executive off rich food and cigarettes. Similarly, when a company sees that it is on the road to bankruptcy, or is facing an unfriendly takeover bid, it can decide that the time has come to do something radical and decisive.

The renewal of many companies (eg Ford, GEC, Jaguar and Olivetti) can be traced directly to a crisis. How do these companies come into crisis in the first place? Usually because they have isolated themselves from the world around them and from their employees, and are not listening to what is going on. Walking around, listening and keeping in touch are basic teamwork concepts, but they are not all that easy to put into practice, even when the necessity is recognised. Listening alone can work wonders. Management should listen to customers, competitors, employees, suppliers, consultants, politicians, etc. They may all have something important to say. And it should be heeded: mere talk is not enough.

INEVITABLE CONFLICTS

The members of a team have to be encouraged to work together: it does not happen automatically. Encouraging very dissimilar people to work together can be a difficult business. Where a difference exists, they must discuss the problem until they arrive at a consensus. Whilst such conflicts are inevitable, they can also be considered to be desirable. An experienced leader will know how to convert conflict into an opportunity, and develop good results from it. Hill and Somers, writing in Cleland and King's *Project Management Handbook* (1985), have shown that the response to internal team conflict varies considerably, depending upon the manager. A good manager will have a large repertoire of responses to such situations, is not afraid of conflict and is willing to meet the problem 'head on'. A weak manager may hope that the problem will disappear of its own accord. Usually it doesn't.

A good team leader, equipped to cope with personality clashes, is prepared to help colleagues cope with interpersonal conflicts. It can also help if someone outside the team intercedes, playing a third-party conciliation role. It is vital to establish a climate that encourages open communication, with the several members of the team able to talk freely to one another. Then conflict can be harnessed to produce positive results.

The members of the team should be told that conflict should never be on a personal level. Differences of view are in themselves good when they relate to the work in hand, and all such differences should be resolved by consensus. Nevertheless there will be times when two rival team members will be seen to be on the verge of an acrimonious outburst. Then any face-to-face meeting should be delayed to allow the participants to 'cool off'. A quiet talk may resolve matters but in extreme cases one or more team members may have to be removed.

To sum up, team leaders have to accept conflict as inevitable, and learn to manage it. The removal of conflicting personalities should be the last resort, since it is never good for the morale of a team to dismiss members once the team has been established.

10 The Approach to Innovation

SUMMARY

We sometimes tend to associate innovation with the individual, but this is by no means always true. Innovation is often the result of teamwork. This comes about because most innovation is not necessarily the result of the brainwave of an individual, but the result of hundreds of minor improvements in design and manufacturing that eventually result in a major breakthrough. Such minor improvements, which finally build up to a leap forward, are normally the result of intensive teamwork, as we demonstrate. We see the Japanese as outstanding exponents of innovation and creativity, largely through most effective teamwork.

THE INNOVATIVE CULTURE

Innovation must be something that seems to happen by accident. Yet it is vital enough to be a basic company objective and needs to be incorporated into the company culture. It seems that most innovation comes from small groups working as a team, and this remains true despite the present rapid growth in technology and the fierce competition that now exists in the marketplace. The present formula for effective innovation seem to be: speed, numbers and the focus on immediate application. Companies in the manufacturing and service sectors are most in need of continuing innovation, and this usually comes through a series of small, application-oriented ideas. Peters (1989) outlines the steps that can be taken in this direction:

- use an explosive number of small starts in order to keep in step with a fast-changing environment, aimed at small markets, and so find a 'niche';
- the focus must be on customer application, and need not necessarily involve a giant leap in technology;
- small independent teams should be set up to attack specific problems, striving to keep ahead of the competitors;
- decentralise as much as possible, treating each project or product as an independent exercise, modifying the approach as it proceeds.

Speaking of the innovative systems developed for the General Motors Saturn project, Chairman Roger Smith observed:

> Where is all this stuff coming from? It's not really coming out of GM . . . it's coming out of little two- and three-man companies, because they're finding out that forty guys can't do something that three people can do. It's just a law of human nature.

It is indeed 'a law of human nature': small teams are extremely effective and management should take advantage of this 'law of human nature'. Roger Smith should be listened to, because he should know what he is talking about. Large firms, of which General Motors is completely typical, cannot be innovative unless they are decentralised and their operations are broken down and handled by small teams. Without teams to develop innovative ideas they are far too slow to move and bring such ideas as they may have into effect. As a result the bias in such companies is towards research rather than practical application. They tend to believe in big projects and elaborate planning systems. The Video Cassette Recorder (VCR) story admirably confirms this.

Giant companies – such as Bell & Howell, CBS, Kodak, Polaroid and RCA – failed in their attempts to develop and sell VCRs. On the other hand, small, relatively unknown companies such as George Atkinson, Andre Blay, Cartridge Television and Massuri Ibuka succeeded, and brought about the VCR revolution. The lesson is there, and it is the larger companies who need to take special note. They should use small teams to develop their projects: it is the innovative way to get things done fast and cheaply. This has been proved time and again, but curiously enough the lesson does not seem to be learnt easily.

Companies continue to grow ever larger – they struggle mightily to grow larger – but to what purpose? This 'think big' attitude of mind must change. Senior executives in particular have to learn to 'think small', and even to 'start small'. But do not think that small companies are automatically successful on this account. The principle is equally applicable to them. Abegglen and Stalk (1985) take us back once again to the Japanese example in this context. They compare Japanese and Western innovation as follows:

> The Kaisha response is often very fast and is offered with a flurry of new product introductions. . . . Most of these [Japanese] innovations are unavailable in the West. . . . [The] common response: 'The Japanese are not using any innovation we are not already aware of . . . our challenge is to 'leap frog' them. [But] the gap that has to be leaped continues to widen, *and the probability of a successful leap continues to fall.*

The emphasis is ours, and it makes the point. Japanese innovation is enabling Japanese industry to draw well ahead of the West, whilst the West is generally too complacent to do anything about it. However, some major companies seem to have listened. At 3M, all the scientists on the staff can devote 15 per cent of their time to a project of their choice; at Hewlett Packard, informal teams are set up for a specific purpose; both IBM and Cray Research have set up duplicate, independent teams to work on a project in parallel, whilst Boeing innovates in parallel with its customers and suppliers, working on small, individual sections or parts of the plane.

WHEN OPPORTUNITY KNOCKS

Innovation and inventions seem to come at random, without planning. At times, the idea seems to come knocking at the door most unexpectedly. Hewlett, back in 1983 when referring to some of the inventions that were the life-blood of Hewlett Packard, maintained that innovation came at random and was completely opportunistic in nature. It seems that this is true of many of the big, well-known commercial and industrial developments. The initial idea often seems to come from unexpected sources, and usually from outside the company that finally develops it. For instance:

- Kodachrome colour photography was invented by some musicians interested in colour photography, and having only a very loose connection with Kodak;

- catalytic cracking of petroleum, a highly efficient method of producing a wide range of fuels, was invented by someone interested in automobile racing;

- the Hewlett Packard HP 3000 computer, developed for scientific use, turned out to be just what the distributed data processing market wanted, leading to that company capturing a major share of the market.

Behind all these random inventions was an innovative team, not necessarily looking for the breakthrough they ultimately achieved. Talking of the relationship between basic research and the actual breakthrough, Ralph Gomory, one-time director of research at IBM, says:

> A breakthrough occurs when the technological knowledge and a way to apply it to meet a need come together in one person's head . . . Incremental steps forward are more pervasive than breakthroughs, but both are important . . . Science can be thought of as a large pool of knowledge fed by the steady flow from the tap of basic research. Every now and then the water is dipped out and put to use, but one never knows what part of the

> water will be needed . . . Yet history shows that
> keeping the water flowing into the pool is a very
> worthwhile enterprise.

Despite the randomness of research, it must be pointed out that in relation to investment in plant and equipment, investment in research is cheap. It is also crucial to continuing innovation, in that it provides the springboard from which so much innovation ultimately comes. It is therefore financially worthwhile: one successful innovative idea will pay for a multitude of research costs.

REWARDING INNOVATION

There is no doubt that those responsible for innovation should be adequately rewarded. It is always true that rewards will produce positive results. Innovators are very valuable people, and deserve encouragement. Here are some typical ways:

- All innovation should be rewarded, whether small or large, significant or insignificant. Whilst financial rewards for innovation are higher in the United States than elsewhere, Japan far exceeds any other country in the number of awards it makes. The premise is that a lot of small awards result in more attempts and suggestions from a wide cross-section.

- Give full support not only to the innovator but also to the team. After all, they have all contributed.

- Make a positive request for innovation, via the 'ideas' box and similar approaches. At a two-day retreat with his top forty officers, a bank president set them the task of providing concrete suggestions that would give 'big savings'. He gave them two hours, and received suggestions that resulted in real savings of some US$700,000.

- The manager must set the example in this, as in everything else. People will do as their manager *does*, not as he says. Notice that this demands that the manager be involved in the innovative process.

In the attempt to secure quick action in relation to innovation, and a reduction in cycle time, there are bound to be failures. In fact, this 'storming' will result in more failures than would normally be expected. But if the proposals that have been made were well thought out, and quickly executed, they must still be rewarded, even though they have failed in practice. Failure, indeed, may not have been the fault of the team making the proposal. There may well be bureaucratic hurdles which should have been removed, or some other cause for failure outside the control of the team. Whilst quick action is basic to successful innovation, it also leads to mistakes. Let us once again heed the masters of the art, the Japanese. Soichiro Honda, the founder of the now world-famous Honda Motor Company, is reported as saying:

> Many people dream of success. To me success can only be achieved through repeated failure and introspection. In fact, success represents the one per cent of your work which results only from that 99 per cent that is called failure.

So don't be afraid of failure: it is the foundation for success. Indeed, quick innovation will inevitably bring a dramatic increase in the rate and amount of failure.

Whilst the objective must be to succeed, it must be accepted that in that process there is bound to be many a failure. But each one should bring its lessons, and the important point is that we should be quick to learn from our failures. As Thomas Edison said after a few thousand failures in his quest for an electric filament bulb that would work: 'I must be much nearer my goal now that I know a great many ways that do not work!' Looking at this problem in another way, failures are the inevitable prelude to success. The sooner you get them behind you, the sooner success will be in your grasp. Remember Honda's assertion that 'success can only be achieved through repeated failure and introspection'. That is, the failure and its reasons must be assessed, and learnt from. We would even suggest that failure should be rewarded: it is so essential to success, and people must not be afraid to fail – therein lies the secret of success!

The acknowledgement and even the encouragement of failure may seem to be contradictory, when the goal is success. There are those who say that you must 'do it right the first time', but this is not a sound management philosophy and it is not practical either, except in the context of production: especially mass production. Some failures may well be due to hurdles that are placed in the way of the innovator, as we have suggested earlier. So management must pay close attention to removing anything that becomes an obstacle: most of them are exceedingly trivial and easily removed. In helping to remove hurdles, management is not only helping the team to get on with their job, it is also signalling to the teams that it means business and is looking for success. This encourages the team to prosecute their work with vigour. Once again, they see that somebody cares – and that in itself can make all the difference.

ROLE OF LISTENING

Innovative companies listen to their employees, their customers and their suppliers. It is a process that never stops. It is amazing how much one can learn merely by listening. Unfortunately, very few of us actually *listen*: we hear, but we do not pay attention to what we hear. But let us make it clear that when we speak of listening, we are not only referring to listening in the normal sense. The good listener goes beyond that, listening between the lines, understanding what is implied as well as what is actually said. Indeed, there are many examples that can be given from industry where listening, especially listening to the customer, has played a most significant role in relation to innovation. The Midland Bank (in the UK) takes pride in calling itself 'the listening bank'. Proctor and Gamble (in the United States) were perhaps the first consumer goods company to publicise a toll-free telephone number, so that customers could phone in their complaints and suggestions without let or hindrance. In just one year (1979) they received some 200,000 calls on their toll-free number, and in the process received a host of useful ideas. Some of these ideas proved to be a major source of product innovation, affecting not only existing products, but also resulting in the introduction of new ones.

This use of the customer can be a success not only in relation to common household items, but also in relation to equipment involving high technology. For instance, it is said of Digital Equipment Corporation, a leader in the development of computers for special applications:

> They rely on customers to find uses for minicomputers, rather than burdening the company with the huge costs of developing and marketing applications on its own. Digital salesmen, engineers selling to other engineers, nurture strong and lasting relationships with their customers.

Indeed, the customer is someone you just cannot ignore. They *are* your business. It is amazing what results simple listening can sometimes bring. What matter that you get asked silly questions: it all helps you to feel the pulse of the market, and that is what market intelligence is all about. The success of IBM is largely due to their ability to listen to their customers, rather than to their technical excellence. As they are quoted as saying of themselves:

> If you're a company of forty thousand people, your normal life is that you are surrounded by other members of the company. You have no natural stimulus from the outside. But somehow or other, we are very conscious of the outside world. We look and worry all the time. That's the basic thing.

It is the things that the competition are doing that are so important. The case is cited of a bank director who reads the annual report of a competitor and is impressed. It is much more revealing than his own report and he asks himself: 'What do they do that we don't? What do they do better than we do?' These may be thought to be naive questions, but they are extremely pertinent, and should not only be asked, but even more important, they should be answered. The answers can often be quite revealing and can lead to company renewal. Such a process of 'listening to others' is not only most useful: it is vitally necessary if a company is to survive and thrive.

Nor should listening be confined to the customer, even though the customer may well have the most important voice. The other voices that can also be significant are those of the suppliers, the distributors, the representatives, the retailers and finally, of course, the company itself. How should one listen? Frequently, systematically and attentively. One should listen not only for facts, but for perceptions and feelings. Obviously those closest to the customer, such as the sales, service and stores people, hear a great deal and they, in turn, should be listened to within their company. New and innovative ideas are sure to be there, waiting to be heard, but it is not all that simple. The good salesman will probe, and has to work hard to get to hear new ideas. There is a great deal of talk about management information systems and their value. Such systems have been getting ever more elaborate over the years and they may well serve a valuable purpose. But what is even more important is the development of a comprehensive customer information system. To be specific, marketing people need to really apply themselves to the acquisition of information from their customers: it should take up at least a quarter of their time, perhaps much more. On this depends the future direction and success of their company.

Listening is closely associated with involvement, and should take place at all levels within the company. This will encourage innovation, which is thereby built into the company culture. It then leads to information sharing, interaction, and recognition. The listening must also be in all directions: those on the work floor should listen to their chairman, and the chairman should listen to the voices on the work floor. Those on the work floor *have* to listen to their foremen, their managers and their chairman: after all, their jobs depend upon it. But the chairman must also listen to what is being talked about on the shop floor. He can then 'feel the pulse' of his people and know what they really think of their work and of their company. This listening can be both formal and informal. The chairman can chat as he walks throught the plant, or there can be extensive formal surveys that end with the production of a formal report. These are all forms of listening. Listening is also encouraged by regular social 'get togethers', a weekly newsletter, videos, celebratory events (such as ten-year service awards) and even small notes of thanks for a job well done.

As for the team leader, he certainly needs to be a compulsive listener. This is the only way in which he can really help his team to succeed in their mission. If the first half of this present century is noted for a type of management that talked down to the employees, hopefully the second half will be noted for managers who are good listeners: managers who leave their offices and walk around to see and hear what is happening and what is being said (shop talk). The manager, and especially the team leader, needs to be completely familiar with the details of the work that his team is doing, being particularly aware of all their problems and frustrations. This enables him to help sort out their problems and so get on with their appointed task.

CREATIVITY AND INNOVATION

Creativity is associated with intuition, and there is the problem of opening an intuitive channel that will support creative behaviour. Despite the apparent randomness of creativity, there is still a constructive approach to problem solving. This can be defined as follows:

- state the problem;

- identify the symptoms: what information can we get?

- gather and share information: what information is needed?

- generate ideas for possible solutions: which is the best?

- combine ideas to build a solution: select between alternatives;

- develop an implementation plan.

Once again, let us turn to Japan for an example. Japan is recognised to be a most innovative country, yet very little of the basic research it uses has originated in Japan. It is usually brought in from some other country. This has left the impression that Japan lags behind so far as creativity is concerned. Yet this really cannot be so, since creativity and innovation are closely linked: indeed interdependent. The Japanese have the knack of capitalising on any innovative or creative idea, wherever it originates, and this is in itself a creative process. This is well illustrated by what Professor Kaoru Kobayashi is quoted by Peters as saying in the course of an interview with the *Japan Times Limited* in 1984:

> When we want to do something, we just try to learn and absorb all possible answers, alternatives and developments not only in Japan, but in Europe, in developing countries, and in the United States. Then, by combining and by evaluating the best of all this, we try to come up with the optimum combinations which are available. We are very *sophisticated copycats*.

The emphasis is ours, and we really do admire such a candid confession. The term 'copycat' has of course long been used in the West for what goes on in Japan, but the professor has not only adopted it, he has improved upon it by prefixing it with the word 'sophisticated', and speaking of it with pride. We ourselves think the term 'copycat' is hardly just, since the Japanese invariably develop and improve upon the ideas and concepts they take over. That is to do much more than just copy: it is not a mere transplant. They are displaying qualities of creativity and innovation, recognising sound ideas and building upon them. The result is that they in the end far exceed the efforts of those who had the original idea, as is clearly demonstrated by their dominance today in markets across the world. It is no wonder that instead of concentrating on the competition at home in the United States, a Ford executive was honest enough to admit: 'Our real competitor is Toyota'.

It seems the West is now beginning to realise that there is no harm and a great deal of benefit in turning 'copycat'. Thus they can repay the Japanese in their own coin. They are adding to the words 'not invented here', 'but swiped from the best with pride'. There is nothing to be ashamed of in taking another's idea and further developing and improving it – displaying creativity and innovation. Professor Kaoru Kobayashi was certainly not ashamed: he was proud, and when we view the commercial success of Japan we can see that he has reason to be proud. One can benefit enormously from the ideas of others, learnt in the marketplace, building upon their hard work and so saving oneself considerable time by not 'reinventing the wheel'. We should all try to become 'sophisticated copycats'.

11 Achieving Success Through Innovation

SUMMARY

Success through teamwork comes in many diverse ways, but innovation is a common denominator, as we now demonstrate by a series of short case studies. Whilst an individual can often do a great deal, a team can do a great deal more. Trophies are won by individuals, but it needs a well-knit and balanced team to win a championship.

ROLE OF INNOVATION

It seems that in the United States the highly innovative team leader has come to be referred to as the 'skunk', and the work of his team as 'skunkwork'. We find this surprising, since the term 'skunk' is not normally used as a nice term or one of praise: rather the opposite. Peters and Austin (1985) explain it as a term borrowed from a comic strip popular in the United States.

It is said that the Lockheed California Company were the first to use it in a business context and that 'Skunk Works' is a registered service mark of theirs. Skunk Works are seen as tiny to modest teams operating in the smaller divisions of the company and performing numerous off-line activities. Whilst the term appears to be used to some extent in a derisory sense, yet there seems no doubt that the operations of the skunk teams are highly prized. For instance, they are described thus:

> . . . it is a highly innovative, fast moving and
> slightly eccentric activity operating at the edges of
> the corporate world . . . often achieving remark-
> able success in arenas that others have written off.

The clue to their success lies in their ability to innovate.
Examples of this ability to innovate abound in industry, and
are well worth study. Let us look at a few.

EXAMPLES OF SUCCESSFUL INNOVATION

One of the best examples is provided by the 'Post-it' note-
pads now to be found in every stationery shop. This innovation has proved a phenomenal success, with a turnover of
some US$200 million for 3M, the company which manufac-
tures the relevant adhesive, but it had a very inauspicious
start.

It is said that a certain Art Fry, who sang in a choir, used
bits of paper to mark the places in his hymn book, but was
perpetually exasperated because they continually fell out.
What was required, he thought, was an adhesive-backed
paper which would stick, but leave not trace when removed. In other words, what was wanted was a rather poor
adhesive: surely that would not be too difficult. Nor was it:
such a product was soon developed. But strangely enough
the market surveys were all negative, and the idea was all
but given up. But then the 3M executives and their secretaries got 'hooked' and hailed it as a breakthrough.

Then the secretary to the chairman at 3M mailed samples
of the new product to the secretaries of *Fortune*, the prestigious American magazine. They got hooked as well, and the
product took off, the 'Post-it' notepad finding a ready
market worldwide. But notice that the breakthrough was
not achieved by the management, but by enthusiastic
employees, and this not until some twelve years after the
idea had first been tabled. Innovation is often not planned.
It can just happen, and sometimes in a very random, hap-
hazard manner.

There are numerous similar examples in industry. The
course of an innovative product, from concept to comple-

tion, usually seems to be messy, unpredictable, and largely governed by the specific qualities of the team leader who is responsible for the project. It seems that the only way to succeed with innovation is by trial and error. Even the notorious Manhattan project, which resulted in the development of the atom bomb, and was acclaimed as a well-thought-out project of strategic importance, was nothing like that. On closer study it is found that what really was happening was that there were competing teams working independently in parallel with a complete lack of coordination between them. But this seems to be the common feature of innovation, and is manifest even in Japanese companies, the past masters in the art of innovation. For instance, Ken Ohmae, the managing director of McKinsey Japan, is reported as saying:

> The Japanese [company] winners look more like survivors of a demolition derby than meticulous strategic planners.

It seems that innovation is inherently a sloppy process. Well, accept that fact and live with it: acceptance can pay enormous dividends. That's the reality, whilst the myth that is commonly believed is just the opposite. Peters and Austin

The myth	The reality
Innovation can be planned	It thrives on uncertainty
A market plan is a must	Move rapidly and experiment
A big team is essential	A small team is far more efficient
Strive for optimisation	Optimisation is a waste of time: it fails in the market
The customer knows what he wants	Innovative product is usually years ahead of the market
Technology brings success	Listening to the market is what brings success

Figure 11.1

(1985) set out the difference between myth and reality as shown in Figure 11.1.

We can see from the set of comparisons that innovation has its own characteristics, and that these will evolve as an innovative project develops. What is going to happen just cannot be foreseen or planned: all in all, it is inevitably a 'sloppy' process.

ACCIDENTAL INNOVATION

A systematic and extensive analysis of 58 major inventions, ranging from the ballpoint pen to the self-winding wrist watch, penicillin, the continuous casting of steel and the digital computer, has demonstrated that some 80 per cent of these ideas actually came from the 'wrong' person, or from a completely unexpected source, ie from the person least expected to produce such an idea. What is more, they often came in the wrong place and even at the wrong time. By way of example:

- Kodachrome was invented by two musicians;
- continuous steel casting was invented by a watch-maker;
- synthetic detergents were inventd by dye-making chemists.

As a result, many of these inventions were initially not readily accepted by the experts in the field. Synthetic detergents were turned down by the soap-making chemists: they had no interest in the idea. Later, all the soap manufacturing companies took up the manufacture of detergents with vigour, and achieved prosperous business. The diesel engine was first developed for railroad use as a convenient engine to haul wagons within railway yards. No one dreamt that it could haul expresses over long distances and thus dominate the transport field. It seems that wherever we look, very little innovation has occurred as or when it was supposed to. Much major innovation was certainly never planned, and this has had the result that much innovative work has taken a long time in commercial development before it reached the user.

One of the myths that has inhibited innovation is the one that asserts that innovation calls for a major project, with a well-integrated group working on it. This is often nonsense. None of the major innovations we have mentioned was the result of major group effort. Rather were they the result of the efforts of a small team, often working unofficially in some quiet corner: moonlighting, as it were.

A typical illustration in this field is the basic oxygen furnace technology developed by Nippin Kokan of Japan. Once perfected and working, it dealt a severe blow to the US steel industry, but was that by design? Not at all. There was a young fanatic in the company who went off on his own to Austria to learn about the basic oxygen furnace experiments going on there. He returned to Japan, put together some outdated equipment and carried out some experiments almost on his own. But it was successful, and his company listened to him. That is of course a characteristic of Japanese companies. Hence their success.

THE INNOVATIVE TEAM

It seems that innovative teams can be a 'pain in the neck'. They certainly need to be handled properly. The best approach is to leave them to their own devices, just ensuring that they have access to necessary resources. The innovative team needs to be nurtured and encouraged rather than managed or controlled.

We mentioned the IBM 360 earlier. This was certainly a major innovative project, developed by a number of *large* teams, working independently and in parallel, but it coped with crisis admirably. Nevertheless, the conviction seems to remain that the best innovative team numbers somewhere between five and 25. And the team needs the right climate. Then they seem to produce what is needed when it is wanted.

It may help to list some of the major characteristics of the truly innovative team: they are not so dissimilar to the characteristics we have outlined for any and every team. The innovative team should:

- be multi-functional;
- be undermanned and overworked;
- have between five and 25 members;
- have members who are all full time;
- have a leader who is outward looking and has a pragmatic thrust;
- have very few rules, and even these should be very simple;
- work for the fun of it, rather than for any financial motive;
- have complete autonomy, including full purchasing authority.

Such a team will normally produce tangible results within from 60 to 90 days.

SELF-MANAGING TEAMS

It is Vogel (1979) who emphasises that the entire business and social structure of Japanese companies is built around the 'Kacho' (section head) and his group of eight to ten team members. These sections are the real building blocks in relation to company management, taking the necessary initiative with the objective of achieving the desired goal. They do this without waiting for an executive order or even for executive support. They are thus a very good example of the 'self-managing team'.

However, though far more widespread in Japan than in the West, the self-managing team was not originally a Japanese idea. It was first seen in military organisation in the West, with the formation of eight-member squads which performed independent tasks. The same concept has since been taken up in industry, with some success. Such teams were often called 'business teams' and were highly autonomous, being made fully responsible for scheduling, training, problem solving and the like. In the early stages it was said that productivity and quality improvement was phenomenal. Tom Peters, in a Foreword to a book by Bob Stramy et al (1985), sets out the reasons:

> The most powerful and influential conclusion concerns the Livonia Planning Team's unqualified support and promotion of the team concept as a central and unifying force throughout the new organisation. So urgent and prominent was the ideal, moreover, that it immediately became the recurrent main theme of the evolving operating plan and its orchestration over the months of planned implementation.

It seems that with the self-managing team the teams are somewhat bigger than we are usually accustomed to: 10 to 30 people. This group gets to know one another extremely well. With the right leadership they learn one another's tasks, and soon achieve group cohesion and a sense of oneness. Because of its size, the group can be self-contained in terms of maintenance, budgeting, inventory management and even customer service. This principle, with a relatively small autonomous group within a big company, can be applied to all the functions within the company, including purchasing and accounting. It is a system of decentralisation, a managerial approach that has always proved highly beneficial.

HIGH-PERFORMANCE TEAMS

Thamhain and Wilemon (1987) conducted a series of research studies, over four years, which have produced very useful guides as to the composition of high-performance teams, of which the innovative team is obviously one version. This field study involved some 30 companies employing over 500 engineering professionals, including 37 managers. All the companies were located in the United States and operated in high technology areas. The prime objective of the research was to demonstrate that 'engineering team performance is associated with drivers and that barriers are related predominantly to (1) leadership and (2) a professionally stimulating work environment'. The results of this most extensive research were documented in five research papers dealing respectively with:

- skill requirements for engineering programme managers;
- professional needs analysis of engineering personnel *versus* performance;
- analysis of barriers to teamwork and potential effects on project performance;
- determination of team performance measures, their drivers and barriers;
- model for developing high-performing project teams.

Some of the major conclusions from this study are:

- effective team building is a critical determinant for project success;
- building the engineering team for a new technical project is a prime responsibility of the programme leader;
- team building requires an entire spectrum of management skills to identify, commit and integrate persons from various functions into a single task group;
- in many engineering organisations, team building is a shared responsibility.

To be truly effective, the project manager must provide an atmosphere conducive to teamwork. The manager needs to integrate people from many different disciplines into an effective team and this requires the creation of a professionally stimulating work environment. There is, of course, a central need for properly qualified team members: the higher the quality of the team, the higher the quality of the information being exchanged. A professionally stimulating environment also has a pervasive effect on the team's ability to cope with change and conflict, and leads to positive performance. When a team member does not feel part of the team and does not trust other members of his team, there is a substantial reluctance to share information. A project leader who knows put it thus:

> There's nothing worse than being on a team when
> no-one trusts anyone else . . . such situations lead
> to gamesmanship and a lot of watching what you
> say because you don't want your own words to
> bounce back in your face.

Effective decision making depends upon team spirit, the ability to trust the information that is becoming available. It also leads to greater individual commitment, with the focus on problem solving. All this results in the development of self-forcing, self-correcting project controls: the main characteristics of a high-performance team.

Where does all this take us? We believe that whilst the study cited above relates to engineering teams involved in high technology, its conclusions relate to *all* teams, whatever their work, whatever the project they may be engaged upon.

THE INNOVATIVE TEAM LEADER

It seems that the leader of an innovative team has to be an outstanding character in some way: it appears he is often classed as weird and even found to be very unreasonable. George Bernard Shaw, in *Man and Superman*, expressed the characteristics of the unreasonable man: the man whom we expect to see leading an innovative team. He wrote:

> The reasonable man adapts himself to the world:
> the unreasonable man persists in trying to adapt
> the world to himself. Therefore, all progress de-
> pends upon the unreasonable man.

The phenomenal success of small companies in meeting market needs, in the face of competition from major companies, seems to lie in the fact that they refuse to acknowledge what everyone else believes to be the reality. And they often succeed. The lesson: learn to recognise and acknowledge the innovative team and the innovative leader. Never despise what they have to say, but rather listen carefully: we can learn much from them.

Also, the innovative leader thrives on challenge. As a

result, projects are taken on with a low probability of success: yet he often succeeds. Machiavelli, writing many hundreds of years ago, said:

> It ought to be remembered that there is nothing more difficult to take in hand, more perilous to conduct, or more uncertain in its success, than to take the lead in the introduction of a new order of things. Because the innovator has for enemies all those who have done well under the old conditions, and lukewarm defenders among those who may do well under the new.

Innovative leaders still have a difficult life, meeting opposition from many quarters. Many questions are asked: Why divert precious resources to a doubtful project? Why work overtime? Why disrupt a production line for a series of speculative experiments? The innovative leader rarely gets whole-hearted support until he has completed his project and it is a demonstrable success.

It has been said that most successful innovators 'have a bit of Honda in them'. This harks back to Honda's founder, Soichiro Honda, a real innovator – full of passion, idealism, pragmatism, cunning, with an enormous impatience with things as they are. Intolerant of any restrictive barrier, the innovative leader is determined to achieve results, at almost any cost, any risk.

PROBLEM SOLVING

We should not leave the subject of innovation without saying something about problem solving, since this is where innovative thinking can often play a substantial role. Any problem is created by a gap that exists between what is and what ought to be. Unless solved, a problem can lead to frustration, anger and anxiety. This, naturally enough, results in lowered output and a fall in productivity. Moreover, a problem left unsolved has a tendency to multiply itself. A positive approach to problem solving is called for, and in the team the team leader should always pay the most careful attention to such problems as are brought forward by the members of the team. Problems should never be ignored or set on one side as unimportant.

In problem solving, the human resource – the ideas of the other members of the team, in particular – should never be ignored. A team leader, concerned with the intellectual process of problem solving, may overlook what is happening in the team in that context. But the team can help, a source of creativity and ideas generation. The leader must:

- listen attentively, and ask for clarification;

- encourage all members to offer suggestions;

- give due recognition to the ideas brought forward;

- recognise that differences in view in the group are good;

- record progress and let the team know.

The fullest cooperation between the members of the team and their leader will usually ensure that the problem is solved. Ulshak *et al* (1981) have written extensively about problem solving, and we can do no better than refer our readers to their book, should they wish to delve deeper.

Part 4

WHO IS TO LEAD THE TEAM?

12 The Project Leader

SUMMARY

What is traditionally called a project manager should be seen as a leader. People want to be led, rather than managed. To be managed implies manipulation, and no one likes to be manipulated. When we come to assess what we expect of a project leader, it seems we are calling for a superman. Some of the necessary qualitites appear to be self-contradictory. We also see that the true leader thrives on change.

SPECIALIST OR GENERALIST?

We can liken the project manager, in the first instance, to the captain of a ship or the commander of an aircraft. Whilst at sea or in the air the immediate need is for quick, effective decisions. Those decisions will often have to be made on the basis of incomplete information or data, but they *have* to be made. What is more, the crew have to implement those decisions without question and without delay, or disaster may result.

Similarly, only a courageous and competent project manager, with a wealth of experience, is really able to fulfil this role. The leader's major contribution, as we shall see, is not technical, but more in the area of 'human relations'. Project managers can and do have a variety of technical backgrounds – usually engineering. But the key to success will lie, not in technical qualifications and capability, but in the ability to handle people.

171

The project manager, the focal point with every project, can make or break a project. The project manager should not rely on his own expertise in, say, engineering. He will have specialists in the concerned disciplines to advise him, and he must rely on them. He must not allow his own specialist knowledge in a certain area to influence his judgment. In fact, he may even be out of date in his own engineering discipline. But what are far more important are the leader's personal qualities. Some of the desirable qualities of a good project manager can be listed:

Adaptable	No-nonsense approach
Benefactor	Organiser
Communicator	Persuader
Delegator	Quietly in command
Enthusiast	Reliable
Flexible	Sensitive
Go-getter	Team builder
Handler of people	Understanding
Initiative taker	Versatile
Jovial	Winsome
Keen	X-ray view
Listener	Yearns for the best
Motivator	Zestful

Some of the qualities may appear to be contradictory, but isn't that what life is all about? One must be kind but firm, to give but one example.

HOTBED OF PARADOXES

The present business environment is in fact so chaotic that Peters (1989) is able to list some 18 paradoxes, large and small; and he says that these are only 'a small sample'. To deal with a paradoxical situation the effective leader has to be unconventional, adaptive and flexible. He has not only to cope with paradoxes but to thrive on them.

Perhaps the core paradox affecting our present assessment of the role of the leader is that *leaders must create internal stability within their teams in order to stimulate constant change and improvement*. The leader needs clear vision to see where he is going, so that risk taking can be encouraged. This is all very necessary if change is to be encouraged. Not only the leader but all the team have to learn to live with paradoxes. Indeed, such paradoxes as are encountered should be discussed openly, each with their practical implications.

THE IMPORTANCE OF LEADERSHIP

The project leader, more than anybody else, is the one able to develop an effective team, by inculcating the right attitude of mind in the team members. Whilst the company should encourage participative management and see that it is put into practice, it is the project leader who actually achieves results. Lock (1987) makes the point that the project leader needs to be fully aware of the problems of human relations and personal sensitivity, constantly on the lookout to prevent personal conflict and to ensure mutual respect amongst the team members.

But the leader is also a member of the team. The respective functions of the leader and the team are different, but completely complementary. The one cannot exist without the other. If the project goals are well defined then all will be working towards a common goal. The last thing we wish to do is to create the impression that it all depends upon the leader.

BEING A LEADER

There is no simple recipe for becoming a leader, but it is also true that leaders *can* be made. An article by Cohen (1989) tells us how to be a leader, and he comments that 'most effective leaders are made, not born'.

In effect, leadership is all about motivation, and most, if not all the traits related to leadership relate either directly or indirectly to the ability to motivate others. Leadership skills can be acquired, but it is a hard road. It is difficult to define the steps in acquiring leadership skills, but a few vital hints are given below.

Show the way

A leader has to be a confident path finder. If he walks with assurance, then others will follow.

Have a compass

It is obviously necessary to lead in the right direction. This means that the leader must know where he is heading: what the objectives are. He has also, of course, to make those objectives clear to his team.

Give due credit

People should always be praised for effort, without fail. If people find that what they do is recognised, then they are encouraged to do even better. This is far more effective than even the most constructive criticism.

Take risks

A leader must be prepared to take risks. All business is fraught with risk and this has to be accepted as the norm. But of course he must learn from failures.

Keep faith

It is crucial that a leader keep faith both with his team and with his superiors. The successful leader trusts others to do well, and then of course they do. The converse is also true: mistrust breeds mistrust. A display of faith in others develops their confidence.

Act the part

An effective leader sounds and looks like a leader. He may well have doubts, but he never allows those doubts to be seen or felt by others. He acts with apparent confidence and assurance. Appearance and manners are always noticed, so these should be polished. Untidiness is to be deplored. A leader should always be unruffled and pleasant company. He should *never* lose his temper.

Delegate

It is most important to delegate work to others wherever possible. This gives others a pride in their work, with a feeling of responsibility. They feel both involved and committed.

Be enthusiastic

Enthusiasm is highly infectious. Once a team is excited about the mission then they will put their very best into the job.

Be competent

The leader cannot know *everything*, but he should know *something* about everything with which he is involved: knowledge is power. The leader should never profess knowledge that he has not got. That is extremely dangerous. If a leader displays competence, the team will look up to him, will look to him for advice and guidance. Maddux (1988) makes the point that team work is vital to the success of any department, and the key to a successful team is effective leadership.

THE LEADER AS TEAM BUILDER

It seems that there are two major types of leadership: transactional and transforming. The transactional leader thrives on making bargains, whereas the transforming leader work on the team, educating and coaching the members. It is the transforming leaders who are chiefly responsible for the renewal of organisations. But a leader, of whatever type, must always be a good team builder. More often than not, the team is inherited from someone else, but then reorganised by the leader, if necessary.

Kotter (1988) argues that creating management teams with *leadership* capacity is far more difficult than building teams that can *manage* well:

If that group lacks certain . . . motives, central
values, or basic skills (which is often the case), no
amount of time and money and effort can change
that fact. . . . One could, of course, recruit an entirely new group of executives who have those
assets, but even the very best potential [outsider]
will not know enough about the company, its culture and its people . . . to develop an adequate implementation network.

It seems that there is no substitute for experience.

Tse (1985) has examined the work of Marks & Spencer in
team building, and offers a valuable insight into how it
should be done. Most of their staff have a relatively high
degree of versatility in terms of both functional and team
roles. To a very considerable extent they are 'generalists',
and this enables the company to combine and recombine
teams with great facility. Marks & Spencer's investment in
training, and in creating the appropriate conditions for
effective team work, has been gigantic, but it is also long-
term. It is seen as a substantial investment in the future. It
has certainly enabled the company to secure a unique
competitive edge, leading to an enviable profit record.
From all this we see that a properly functioning team is one
in which people:

1   Really care for one another.

2   Are completely open and truthful.

3   Have a high level of trust between themselves.

4   Decide issues by consensus.

5   Have a strong team commitment.

6   Face a conflict together and work it through.

7   Really listen to one another's ideas and feelings.

8   Express their own feelings freely.

But behind all this there remains one person, the leader,
usually in the background, rejoicing in the achievements of
the team.

The leader needs to ensure that team members:

- are proud of belonging to the team;
- are adept at their work;
- like their work and enjoy the risks;
- have a feeling of power and success;
- are rewarded with praise for good work;
- receive the appropriate financial reward.

Toft (1988) writing of his own personal experiences as a project manager over some twenty years, puts effective leadership at the head of the requirements for a successful project manager. It is very necessary, he asserts, for the project team to have confidence in their collective ability to cope with all the problems that come. This demands tolerance and trust between team members, and it is the leader who has to ensure that this exists.

It seems that it is the team, rather than the individual, which is going to achieve sustained and enduring success in management, since it is a storehouse of collectively owned experience, information and judgment. Power and authority is now vested in the team, rather than any specific individual. An individual is prone to make mistakes, but the team has a greater spread of knowledge and experience: so mistakes are far less likely.

LEADERS THRIVE ON CHANGE

Change is inevitable. One can either complain about it, accept it or adapt to it. Best of all, one can thrive on it. That is precisely what a good leader will do. Change can be very unsettling and even chaotic. No wonder then, that we find the word 'chaos' in the title of a book by Peters (1989) purporting to be a handbook to guide us through the management revolution. In his Preface he shares with us the problem he had in selecting a suitable title. He felt that both the words 'chaos' and 'thrive' were very relevant, but should the title be 'Thriving *amidst* chaos', or 'Thriving *on* chaos'? He finally decided on the latter. Writing of the changing times we now face, he says:

... this book is about a revolution – a necessary revolution. It challenges everything we thought we knew about managing, and often challenges over a hundred years of American tradition. Most fundamentally, the times demand that flexibility and love of change replace our long standing penchant for mass production and mass markets, based as it is upon a relatively predictable environment now vanished.

Leaders working in companies that accept and welcome change – renewing companies they are called in the literature – themselves welcome change, accept it and treat it as normal. This takes away much of the fear and anxiety associated with change. They even use the opportunities it creates and thus thrive on it! From the multitude of examples we could quote, let us just mention one: Dick Huber of Citicorp, as quoted by Waterman (1987). He said:

When things are growing we can make a bundle: when things are shrinking we can make a bundle. We thrive on change. A turbulent environment plays to our strengths . . . Citicorp manages by shuffling the deck once in a while, and we do it when we aren't in trouble. Reorganize on the crest of the wave, not when you are down in the trough.

Surely that is to 'thrive on chaos'. Or, better, to thrive on change, for change has a much more positive connotation than chaos.

13 Profile of a Project Leader

SUMMARY

The previous chapter sought to set out the profile of the leader who is also an effective project manager. We saw that he had to have a whole range of attributes, some contradictory. Now we look at some of these qualities more closely and illustrate them with real-life examples from past projects.

THE LEADER CAN MAKE THE DIFFERENCE

There is no doubt that an effective leader can make all the difference in relation to project success or failure. Recognition of this fact is crucial to successful team building. Proper selection of the leader is essential. Main (1987), for instance, in an article with the title, 'Wanted: leaders who can make a difference', comments that 'mere management isn't good enough any more' and explores 'how companies are trying to turn out executives who can transform organisations and create a corporate future'. Companies are looking for people like Lee Iacocca of Chrysler or Jack Welsh of General Electric. The achievements of these men have been acclaimed in the media, but there are many more 'unsung heroes'. Appointed to the highest office in his company in 1981, Jack Welsh feared that he would be 'abrasive', but he proved to be a model leader. An intuitive revolutionary, he preached and practised the concept: 'If it ain't broke, fix it', a radical departure from the conventional wisdom, 'If it ain't broke, leave it'. Welsh loved change and in the process got rid of a number of unprofitable, low-growth enterprises, concen-

179

trating on those that were doing well. This was a radical departure from previous policy. In the process he eliminated more than 10,000 jobs and revitalised General Electric. It is this type of leader that transforms an organisation, creating a brighter and better future for the company, its employees, its suppliers and its customers.

The subject of leadership has assumed great prominence in the management literature over recent years. There is even a chair of leadership (named after Konosuke Mutushita) at the Harvard Business School.

We have always maintained that leaders, usually, are not born, but are 'made'. Leaders can be trained to do the job very effectively, but such training is best carried out 'on the job'. At college or on courses you can teach managers to be more imaginative, to communicate better and to be more self-aware. But you cannot teach them to exercise sound judgment, thrive on chaos, work with energy and be curious about all that happens. That only comes with practical experience.

Nevertheless there are a number of courses that seek to teach leadership. The Wharton School, in the United States, started its first course on leadership late in 1987. The dean, Russell Palmer, set the course in motion even though his faculty colleagues insisted that this is one subject that cannot be taught. The first such course was probably the one instituted in 1984 by the North Western University Business School. Since then many other business schools have followed suit and such courses are growing ever more popular. The Center for Creative Leadership at Greensboro, North Carolina, reported that the number of its students, sponsored mainly by corporations, had tripled over the last five years. In order to drive home the leadership lessons, management games have been devised. Typical of these is the 'boat exercise', which demonstrates that it is very hard to get thing right whilst the managers keep meddling. The moral is that to be a good leader you must leave your team alone to get on with their work, holding merely a watching brief and ensuring a positive and supportive working environment.

Zanger (1985) makes the point that leaders should provide visionary inspiration, motivation and direction. Leadership generates an emotional connection between the leader and those who are led. There is no doubt that effective leadership attracts people and inspires them to remarkable efforts in a common cause.

One can draw an interesting parallel in this context with the educational world, and the role of the teacher. A leader is very like a teacher, and there are degrees of leadership, just as there are great differences in the ability of teachers. The gradations can be set out as follows:

The Leader or Teacher	Action
Mediocre	Tells
Good	Explains
Superior	Demonstrates
Great	Inspires

The distinction between a manager and a leader, although rather subtle, is becoming clearer as the significance of leadership in management is becoming more widely recognised. If we see leadership as something different to management, we then recognise that there are a number of leadership styles, which we have sought to set out in Figure 13.1. This presentation is undoubtedly an oversimplification. We show the main features of the various styles of leadership, but there is a considerable overlap both in leadership style and in the various schools of management.

ROLE OF THE PROJECT LEADER

The project manager, or project leader, is in effect the head or chief executive of a 'temporary company'. He is involved in setting up what amounts to a new company with a limited, specific life span. That life span extends from the conception to the completion of the particular project. His team is drawn from elsewhere: usually largely from the various departments within the company. Often, of course, specific individuals are 'hired in' to complement the team. This means that all the members are 'on loan', deputed to

		SCHOOLS OF MANAGEMENT		
Function	Scientific	Bureaucratic	Human relations	Behavioural science
Production	Linestaff Close control Rewards and punishment People are commodities	Systems Regulations Technology Traditional values People are involved in decisions	Cooperative participation Happy family is a productive family Comfort and fringe benefits	Best results through achievement of individual goals Team Management
Decisions	Management	Informal, negotiating	Employees	Shared, but management is accountable
Role	There is a boss of a 'tight ship'	Technician Salesman Compromiser	There is a father figure	Team handler Coach Change agent
Motivation	Good working conditions Loyalty and expectation	Status Achievement Recognition	Involvement Acceptance	Team involvement Self management and actualisation
Feelings	Keep feelings etc out of work situations	Controlled, but low key	People want what they get	Creative ideas will overcome hangups
Communications	Get instructions	Openness Information programmes	Openness Accentuate the positive	Two-way dialogues

Figure 13.1

work on the project for the duration – and all the team members know this very well. A project can last from a few months to several years; most projects last two to three years.

The project places all the members of the project team, often with their families, in completely new surroundings, sometimes in another country, for the period: a period usually significant to the individual in terms of career development. At the end of the project they will either return to their former department, or go on to the open market, usually with another project in view. Whatever happens, they will expect to be upgraded after a period of some years. All this constitutes a very special environment in terms of career development, creating strains which the project manager has to recognise and deal with. It is necessary to consider the future of each member of the team and to ensure, as far as possible, that they *have* a future. Otherwise, as the project proceeds, the team members will be ever less enthusiastic about their present work (see Figure 13.2).

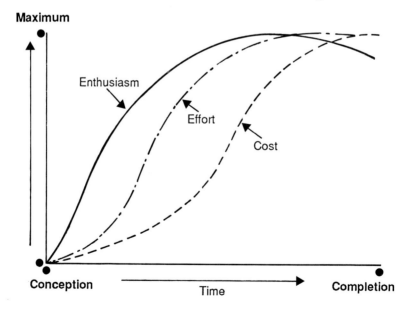

Figure 13.2

Compare this situation with that of an individual coming up to retirement age. Very few in that position maintain their enthusiasm right to the bitter end, working with vigour till the day they retire. The normal situation is for enthusiasm to fall off markedly over the last six months or so. Now six months is not a lengthy period in terms of a person's working life, and such a situation can be accepted by management, but six months is usually a very significant period in the life of a project, and such a fall-off in effort could do considerable harm to the project. It is one task of the project manager to prevent this.

LEADING BY EXAMPLE

Bechtel, a major worldwide company in the construction industry (often the first and always in the first five companies listed in the *Top 400 Contractors* in the United States, published annually in *Engineering News Record*) has some 350 project engineers on its staff. From time to time the sayings and doings of some of these project managers are publicised and their comments on their work can be most helpful. For instance, one issue of *Bechtel Briefs*, the company house magazine, featured the project manager responsible for the world's largest Liquid Natural Gas (LNG) project, and he is quoted as saying:

> The role of a project manager is essentially to keep an objective view of the whole project – its trends, problems and activities – from an informed viewpoint. It's important that the project manager does not become, for example, the engineering manager or the construction manager on the project, but stands back and ensures that engineering and construction are properly performed and managed.

Another project manager, with more than thirty years of experience behind him, describes himself as a firm believer in 'cooperative management'. We have already demonstrated the way in which the Japanese, in particular, have developed cooperative management into a fine art. This project manager explains the principles of cooperative management thus:

> Generally, people are interested in performing well and cooperating if they are treated like human beings and not criticized unnecessarily ... You've got to compliment people on their good efforts and performance, you've got to work with them, put forth the effort to help them work well with one another. If you're going to get the job done well, it will be through teamwork and cooperation, not through fighting with one another.

Notice that the same lessons are being brought forward time and again. It is a simple message, but it needs to be listened to and then brought into constant practice. Let us take one last lesson from this project manager with such extended experience. He recognises that people want to feel that they are part of a team: that they are really producing and achieving something. How do you do this? He tells us:

> You have to be a good listener and respect the thoughts and ideas of the project team members. Then you have to be able to evaluate this input and provide appropriate direction. You have to be able to recognise capability in individuals and give them every opportunity to use their initiative. The younger people of today are going to be the managers of the future and we must help them gain experience. Technical training is essential, but I don't think you can be highly technical or theoretical and be a good project manager on that basis.

He goes on to say that 'if you manage too much, you'll stifle initiative. If you give good people a free rein, you're stimulating their initiative. I learned these lessons from the best people in the business'. In fact, McGinnis (1985), writing of the way in which one can bring out the best in people, puts it thus:

> The ultimate leaders develop followers who will surpass them. Runners will become coaches and

train other athletes who will break their records. Executives will motivate subordinates so successfully that they will become their superiors. And parents, in their devotion to a child, will pull him or her up beside them – and then encourage the child to go even higher.

In all the above quotations we have a variety of recurrent themes, all of which have come before us time and again as we have pursued the theme of the value of teams, and the role of the team leader. Words and phrases such as 'learning', 'initiative', 'experience', 'being a good listener', 'teamwork' and 'cooperation' recur constantly. These are the essential elements in a good team, led by an effective project manager.

CONSULT AND COOPERATE

We have already seen that consultation and cooperation play a major role in the successful team, and must therefore be cultivated by the project manager. We have to recognise that almost invariably the project team is created for the purpose in view, and will be disbanded once the project has been completed. There is no reason at all why a group of individuals, brought together in this way to form a team, should automatically function together effectively, however excellent they may be, each one, as individuals. For a team to work together as a team it is necessary for the attributes of the individuals and their tasks to be properly matched, and for the several tasks within the team to be properly correlated.

The team concept has been challenged, particularly in the running of companies. It has been said that the 'team concept' challenges the effectiveness of the role of the chief executive. On a project *within* a company the project manager is the 'chief executive'. The project manager should make the final decision when necessary and lead, yet he should work with and through his project team. In passing, that is equally true of the chief executive of a company. There should be both cooperation and consultation between the various team members, both inside and outside the formal meetings.

It is said that, particularly in company management, natural social reticence thrives on understatement, that people tend to speak with innuendo, or in code, and that it is very difficult to break this down. There is no doubt that this is true, and that enormous effort is called for on the part of management to break away from this mode of working, but that effort should be made. Barriers that exist between the workforce and the management *must* be broken down. The current class system in Britain, which recognises two distinct groups – management and workers – creates conflict and inevitably reduces overall performance. This must not happen with the project: it is the task of the project manager to see that such a division into class groups does not occur. Once a decision has been reached, *everyone* in the team should be fully committed to that decision, support it loyally and implement it without any reservations.

Let us illustrate the point by a practical example from the construction industry. Lummus Canada once received a contract from Esso Chemical Canada and during construction of the plant the two companies developed what was considered to be a unique integration of their field staffs. They were actually driven to it by a shortage of skilled personnel. The Esso personnel on site constituted some 30 per cent of the total site administration: Lummus personnel the other 70 per cent. But they *all* reported to the Lummus Canada Construction Manager. This integration was not the result of some grand design, but evolved from a series of *small* steps taken by the respective project managers. There was single, rather than dual reporting to management, and as a result a 15 per cent saving was made on the originally estimated requirements for technical manpower on the project. But what is more important, there were better site relations and completion was speeded up. The staff even traded their respective 'hard hats': Esso wore blue and Lummus white, thus demonstrating their unity of purpose.

This experiment in cooperation remains an outstanding

example of owner/contractor cooperation. The knitting together of personnel from two very different companies was the right way to build a team. This required exceptional leadership qualities – which are not all that common.

THE ACTION-CENTRED LEADER

Managers should be noted for the quality of their leadership, a skill which can and must be acquired. This cannot be left to chance. Some may learn faster than others, but training is required and should be sought. Such training comes best from those who have experience and can impart it to others. In the ultimate analysis, managers will be judged by their effectiveness as leaders. This largely depends on:

- ensuring that allotted tasks are completed on time;

- creating and building a team that can deal with the task ahead;

- developing the team members by coaching, guidance and training;

- being quite clear about the task ahead, and making this clear to the team;

- understanding and explaining the way in which the task fits in with company objectives;

- planning with the team how the task is best accomplished; determining and then obtaining the necessary resources, indeed human resources;

- closely monitoring project progress;

- appraising the project following upon completion, to learn the lessons.

The foregoing qualities should all be demonstrated by the action-centred leader. Adair (1986) defines an *action-centred leader* as follows:

Action-centred leaders are enthusiastic, capable of encouraging and inspiring others by word and

> example. They have an understanding of people, and learn their leadership and skills by doing leadership actions . . . What you need to do to be a leader: motivation, target setting and appraisal; delegation and decision taking; effective use of time; training, and managing change. The action-centred leader is about learning by doing. If this sounds like simple common sense, it is. But it is up to the action-centred leader to put common sense into common practice.

He speaks as though the action-centred leader is a class apart, but of course *all* leaders, all managers, should be action centred.

Effective leadership is nothing more than plain common sense. However, many leaders are completely unable to motivate their team members through encouragement and inspiration by word and by example. Perhaps they do not try, never having appreciated the need. People are self-motivating, but the opportunity has to be presented to them: self-motivation has to be encouraged.

The participation of the team members must be real and put into practice through delegation and decentralisation. This is the responsibility of the leader, and the action-centred leader will see that it happens. People and time, as the most precious resources, should be used economically and effectively. This is the crux of good management, good leadership.

14 The Need for Vision

SUMMARY

*Project execution calls for very close attention to detail. The project leader himself is not directly concerned with detail: that is the responsibility of others. Yet he must be broadly aware of the detail. He must certainly be looking ahead towards the completion of the project immediately in hand, but he has to look further than that. He must have vision. He has to look ahead to what is going to come after, both for himself and for all the members of the team. They **all** must have a future.*

ROLE OF DELEGATION

A manager copes by telling people what to do, but the true leader empowers his team, so that they can get on with their respective jobs without reference to him. The proper way to empower people is by delegation, but there are few managers who can and do truly delegate to others. They always seem to want to hold a watching brief, and display doubt as to whether those to whom they have delegated a task are able to do it effectively. The true leader will delegate so that his staff have complete freedom to initiate action without reference to him. True delegation means that the leader has really let go: there is no holding back, no restraining influence, no constant checking. Of course, the appropriate standards must have already been set: one can only delegate to those who are competent. That has to be established first of all.

There should be no formal controls once a task has been delegated to another: only quiet cognisance of what is happening just in case something goes wrong. The leader has to be very careful once a task has been delegated not to intervene, even inadvertently. This is so easy: the casual question can be interpreted as interference. Complete delegation sounds a little like anarchy, but it isn't.

LOOKING TO THE FUTURE

It is important to realise that no one knows what the future holds. To illustrate the ignorance of even the professionals, the journal *Long Range Planning* once devoted an entire issue (August 1982) to this subject, with several articles under the main heading 'Corporate Planning for the Uncertain Future'. The reasons for uncertainty were many, but the leading article made the point that, whilst planning has traditionally been based on hunch, life is now so complex that the *forecaster* is called in. Then, the writer says, 'He, in his turn, realizes that he cannot provide a single line answer without qualifications. The qualifications get lost on the way to the decision maker and so the process becomes mechanistic.'

Almost all forecasting is based on current trends, and we would contend that any forecast so based must always be suspect. The oil crisis of 1973 offers us an outstanding example. There had been steady industrial growth across the world for some 30 years, ever since World War Two, but this upward curve collapsed overnight. The corporate plans of thousands of companies collapsed with it. Yet there are still those who analyse current trends, then make projections and predictions – and there are still those who listen to them with close attention.

Even accepting that the future is uncertain, it is still worthwhile to assess the prospects for the project leader and his team. We have already seen that it is essential to have a short-term assessment of the possibilities: the project leader and his team have to have some idea as to what will happen to them when the project comes to an end. They need to be able to look with some assurance to that immediate future, if their present work is not to be adversely affected.

This is a very real problem when people are working on projects abroad. Every year there are more and more companies operating on a multinational or even global basis, with offices and factories in other countries. Inevitably personnel are posted from the home country, usually to take up a managerial role. Their task is to introduce the company techniques and knowhow in the distant location. It is always a difficult assignment, since a posting to another country, usually with another language and very different customs, can create a very stressful situation. Those who get on best are those who are able, although expatriates, to make their new location their *home*. Unfortunately, many expatriates seem to spend a lot of their time thinking about what is going to happen when they 'go back home' again: this is another aspect of looking to the future.

Buchanan (1985) makes the point that when such people return home it is very difficult to get them back into the stream, especially when the home base is contracting in size, as is today so often the case. Based on their own experience, the Swedish car group Volvo has now designated someone at Head Office to communicate regularly with its executives abroad to let them know what is happening at home, especially in relation to job opportunities. This has not only reassured the expatriates – at long last they feel that somebody back home cares – but it has helped in their placing when they finally return. Once again we see the importance of seeing people as people, with feelings and emotions that need to be satisfied if they are to do a good job.

There is a real shortage of competent managers who can be sent abroad. Murray (1986) points out that whilst the United States were pioneers in this area, their failure rate is much higher than that of the Japanese. Another survey showed that over 75 per cent of the 80 US corporations who responded found that between ten and 40 per cent of their personnel assigned abroad had to be recalled or dismissed, because of poor performance, although their home record had been excellent. The Japanese corporations, however, reported very differently. Of the 35 who replied, 86 per cent reported a failure rate of less than ten per cent, and in no case did the failure rate reach 20 per cent. The reason for this difference appears to lie in the fact that Japanese companies are willing to invest much more heavily in training and support of their expatriates.

But despite the problems, there is no doubt that project managers with their teams will still be required. Progress is still being made in the developed world, whilst in the developing world one can reasonably expect significant advances to be made, as those involved become ever more aware both of their needs and their shortcomings. Baker (1982) expects considerable changes in techniques until the turn of the century, in terms not only of the tools available and the techniques employed, but also in the type of project that will have to be handled. He pleads for more systematic research to identify the variables that contribute to project failure in a variety of settings, if only to minimise such failures in the future. The three factors that he says can help are better logistic support, improvement in morale and a significant improvement in the language skills of project managers.

At one time, project managers running international projects came almost exclusively from the United States and Western Europe, but now the developing countries are beginning to dominate the international scene. South Korea and Turkey are the most recent examples of this movement, but they are not alone. They are now being joined by others: notably Mexico, China and India. We are also seeing the steady transformation of the manager into the leader. Whilst the manager fears and avoids change, the leader will encourage it and thrive on it. Whilst the manager is absorbed in repetitive and routine tasks, the leader will be innovative and visionary.

THE PROJECT ENVIRONMENT

Another aspect that is becoming ever more important is the need for business skills in the project environment. The project leader now needs to be a businessman as well as a human relations expert. He will need to develop an understanding of financial controls, human motivation and administration (both legal and general business administration), and put that understanding to good use.

The human element is becoming ever more important, ever more crucial, and this is justification enough for our sub-title: 'the human factor'. People, already accepted by many companies as the most precious resource they have, are likely to become ever more important.

There is a trend towards the concept of looking after the employee in places other than Japan, but it is coming too little and too late. Time and again a successful, profitable company will close down a factory, to the devastation of the location where that factory is sited, just because its return is below average. Whilst the protective policy and the 'backward areas' development practised for instance in India, which result in a multitude of 'sick' companies, may be going to the other extreme, they have a very proper objective: the protection of the weak and helpless in society. The Japanese have their own unique way of handling this problem. As Dr Ito says, 'firing employees is good for nobody', so they don't do it. Yet they remain prosperous and make profits. Their technique, if there is a labour surplus, is to switch to another product or service, and train the workforce as appropriate.

Summing up, let us emphasise yet again that one man, alone, can achieve very little. The desired end is in fact achieved by a multitude of workpeople and their several leaders, often scattered far and wide, in many countries. We have seen that Japan can provide us with many illustrations and sound lessons in relation to good management and that essential element in good management: good leadership. So let us bring this section on the role of the project leader to a conclusion on a somewhat philosophical note by quoting Masao Kamei, the chairman of the Sumitomo Electric Industries Ltd of Japan. He was speaking at a management seminar held in February 1986 at the Keidanren Kaikan in Tokyo. He looked first at the qualities necessary in the leader, saying:

Of all the qualitities necessary for good leadership, I think that personal magnetism – charisma
– is most important. Napoleon, Oda Nobunaga
and Toyotomi Hideyoshi were all a far cry from
exemplary 'managers' and they would probably
have received failing marks in that sense. But what
they all possessed was an overwhelming personal
magnetism which more than offset their shortcomings. A person with great magnetism is one
who induces others to come to him for advice and
assistance.

This seems to say that good managers, or perhaps excellent
managers, are born rather than made, but we, amongst
many others, cannot agree with this. The lessons that we
have developed and the examples we have given of the
effective leader and team builder demonstrate that leadership can indeed be learnt and applied.

Part 5
TEAMS IN ACTION

15 Examples from the United States

SUMMARY

Part 5 consists of three chapters, each of which presents a series of real-life case studies to demonstrate the way in which teamwork has been used successfully across the world. Practical example is so much more convincing than mere discussion. In this chapter we take our examples from the United States. We look at the way in which a number of US companies have successfully applied the principles of teamwork, including IBM, Ford and General Motors.

IBM SYSTEM 360

IBM is by far the largest computer company in the world, with sales approaching US$60 billion a year. They are followed, but not closely, by DEC and a number of other companies. But the sales of these companies range between US$3 and 12 billion a year. No wonder this situation has been described as 'Snow White and the seven dwarfs'. But how has 'Snow White' achieved such a dramatic success? If we were to seek to sum up the primary reason, we would point to the fact that the company has complete faith and trust in its employees as people.

The greatest asset in the company is the *man*, not the *machine*. Perhaps, intentionally or otherwise, they have created what we can term the 'Japanese culture' within their company, although they operate outside Japan. This faith and trust in people extends, of course, to the project teams that are set up to achieve specific objectives. One such was the development of the IBM System 360, a project that not only established IBM as leader in the computer field, but has assured a bright future for the company for a long while to come. Nevertheless, the company is by no means resting on its laurels.

IBM came into existence in 1924 as the successor of CTR (Computer-Tabulator-Recording), a company founded by Charles Flint in 1910. The man who set the tone of the company, however, was Thomas Watson. His basic philosophy, which seems to have been preserved as part of the 'company culture' right down to the present day, was expressed thus:

> A company is known by the men it keeps. We have different ideas, and different work, but when you come right down to it there is just one thing we have to deal with throughout the whole organisation – that is the *man*.

(That was said, of course, before women began to play such an important role in industry: perhaps today he would have chosen different words.)

Whilst emphasising the importance of the individual, Watson also strongly stresses the importance of teamwork:

> A team that won't be beat can't be beat . . . Everybody in this company is the supervisor of someone else . . . no man is big enough to instruct everybody how to do his work.

Whilst we are going back some seventy years, Watson's view is still valid – the emphasis being on teamwork and the importance of giving both the individual and the team full opportunity to use their skills in order to achieve success.

The development of System 360 is a supreme example of teamwork in action. The principal architect was Frederick Brooks, but he had a very large support team. Peters and Waterman (1984) tell us that those in the team with managerial functions met once a week for a half-day conference to review progress, and contact between the team members was continuous and intense. Minutes of such meetings were circulated within a few hours and every member of the team had instant access to all the information that he required. This sharing of information went right through to the programmers, who received copies of material from every group within the project team. In addition, there were annual two-week sessions, where all outstanding problems were resolved. Everyone attending the weekly meetings had the authority to make binding decisions on behalf of their departments. We are told that Frederick Brooks continually emphasised the necessity for open communications. With a giant project team and a much larger than normal task force, there had to be a field structure, which was reorganised regularly, but all members of the team had access to *all* the information required by them. In the context of what we have said so far in this book, all this sounds normal enough, but it was a unique management procedure at the time.

The development of System 360 cost more and took longer than had been expected. But it has to be remembered that IBM were working on a development project in a high technology area, and this can involve many unknowns. In their anxiety to pre-empt their competitors, they proclaimed as early as 1962 that the system would be available by April 1964. But at that point in time the system was still being developed. In addition, development costs were escalating. However, whilst the first 360/40 computers were installed in April 1965, a year later than had originally been planned, they were an instant success.

Before the end of that year other models in the series – the 360/30s, 50s and 60s – had also appeared and there was a record backlog of orders for this new series of machines. The production problems had been surmounted and the transition from what was called 'second generation' to 'third generation' computers had gone very smoothly indeed. Within two years the 360 series accounted for nearly half of the total sales of IBM at home and the series was also making great strides abroad, with sales far ahead of those of any of its competitors.

Whilst the competition was well aware of what was happening and was developing its response, no one was ready to enter the market when the 360 appeared. The development of a new generation in computers is both expensive and time-consuming, and it was thought that such a major technological advance would take at least ten years. IBM got there in less than half that time, such is the power of teamwork! But whilst the 360 series has been the dominant factor in the growth of IBM over the past decade, the company has not stopped there. It is suggested that it may well become the world's biggest corporation. It already employs more than 40,000 people worldwide, and Harris (1985) outlines a most prosperous future for the company, estimating that the annual turnover will increase to some US$100 billion by 1990.

However, what we wish the example of IBM to illustrate and emphasise is that the project team concept is *always* the answer, whatever the size of the company. Problems, whether they be direct manufacturing problems, or the introduction of a new product, as it was with IBM, should always be formulated as a project, with a stated objective, to be achieved within a budgeted cost and within a stipulated time. Then a group of people should be nominated, with a leader, to produce the answer.

TEAMS EVERYWHERE

Peters and Austin (1985) introduce us to a very wide variety of companies who have tackled a host of very different problems by the effective use of teamwork. For instance, Milliken & Co, the US$2 billion textile powerhouse at Spartanburg, South Carolina, and always a technology leader, incorporated an amazing quality improvement programme into their system in 1980, and moved from an authoritarian management structure to one where quality enhancement was obtained by giving their employees management participation. Their quality programme has been hailed by the experts in this field as one of the most advanced in the United States: but our point is that it is based on participative teamwork.

Campbell Soups and the Pepsi Company are two very well-known companies, with a worldwide reputation, that for years have avoided stagnation in their management system by revitalising the company with entrepreneurial programmes that can serve as models for the rest of industry. At the heart of their success has been complete decentralisation of the company, with the setting up of independent profit-making centres which use teams in every phase of their work. In sharp contrast to this managerial approach, we have the comment of General Bill Creech, of the US Air Force Tactical Command: 'Centralisation is the enemy!' Yes, and the larger the company, the greater an enemy it becomes.

To take an example from a more unusual field, Lockheed's Kelly Johnson took up a challenge in relation to an ailing satellite enterprise. The project was some two years late, and the cost was well above the budget. What did he do? The number of inspectors working for one subcontractor was trimmed from 1271 to 35. By efforts such as these, which demanded the setting up of quality teams, the programme was brought back on schedule. On two other United States Air Force projects of similar size Lockheed was on schedule and under budget, employing 126 people on the project. On the other hand, a competitor employing 3750 people on the project was several years behind the planned programme and well off budget. These examples demonstrate that teams, even small ones, can really work wonders. And often, more people mean less work.

There is no doubt that successful companies, such as the ones cited, achieve their success through teamwork and proper management. They do far better than their competitors, even in declining markets. Instead of blaming their problems on others, these companies seized the opportunity and used the situation to their benefit. It is worth citing also the following examples, showing the excellence – and increased profits – that come with the intelligent use of teams:

-   Du Pont's safety record is 68 times better than the manufacturing industry average in the United States.

- The firm Frank Perdue, with a 60 per cent market share, earns a margin per pound of chicken, which is several hundred per cent above the industry average.

- Stew Leonard's sales per square foot of dairy products are fully ten times the industry average.

- Mervyn's remerchandises a US$1.25 billion operation a dozen times faster than its competitors.

However, not all companies, either in the United States or elsewhere, seem to have taken the teamwork concept to heart. Two of the major weaknesses with companies in the United States have been said to be:

- a failure to encourage teamwork;

- excessive management.

In a way, these two faults are related, since the encouragement of teamwork through decentralisation, and the development of teams, will inevitably weaken management at the centre. Hence a company operating with teams will automatically have less management. There is no doubt that remarkable results have been achieved when a company has made a postive effort to decentralise its operations, placing the power and the authority at what we might call the action level – with the teams themselves.

In the United States a wide variety of expressions have been developed to describe this particular management style. Dividing people into teams is described as 'chunking', the teams then being described as 'bits and pieces', 'champions', 'project centres', 'quality circles', 'skunkworks', 'task forces' and the like. It seems that although the team concept is basic to successful management, and although a team is the most vital building block in the company organisation, the team concept never shows up on the company's organisational chart. That still follows the familiar hierarchical pattern. Yet so many major companies do it. For instance:

- The Control Data Corporation established SWATS (Special Workforce Action Teams), each of which concentrates for 90 days on jobs previously done by outside contractors, such as painting, plumbing and general maintenance.

- The company CRS Sirrine regularly uses teams consisting of six to eight architects, who work on three to six different projects at a time. Each person thus gets exposed to many different facets of the company's business.

- In Delco Remy everyone is either a team member or a support person, such as a plant manager. Each team selects its own leader, whilst a line supervisor acts as an 'advisor', dealing with routine problems. There are also weekly meetings to set out the goals for the following week.

- General Mills operates groups of teams, with each team working on a brand-name product. Each team thus gets involved in all facets of the manufacture and marketing of that product, including distribution and advertising.

- The company 3M uses what they call New Venture Teams, each team being essentially a task force that plans and then develops a new product. If the product looks profitable, then a division is set up to manufacture and market it.

- At Western Electric over 15,000 of its employees are organised into permanent Quality Circles (see Chapter 20). These teams are doing what is called 'skunkwork': they identify, analyse and solve unit-related problems.

This is a long list, and it could be longer. Let us finish by mentioning the R G Boerg Corporation, a footwear manufacturer, that organised its 300 employees into teams of 8–12 people, each team being responsible for the manufacture of a specific product, starting with the raw materials. In addition, these teams participate in the overall company decision-making. This brought about a complete transformation within the company. The employees felt *involved* and committed to their company. They felt they had a say in their own future.

Some companies have really integrated the team concept into their company structure. With Intel it even finds a mention in the company's statement of philosophy, thus:

> Teams are an integral part of the Intel work ethic environment. Team performance is critical to the accomplishment of Intel objectives...Team object-ives take precedence over individual objectives. This principle is applied in day-to-day operations and is fundamental. [Any] changes are made in a manner to optimise team results, rather than to maintain individual career paths.

This statement is very clear: the team and its objectives are paramount – and so they should be!

When we look around for outstanding 'leaders', we see that Iacocca is credited with having turned Chrysler around single-handed, and the same is said of Sir Michael Edwardes in relation to British Leyland. But this cannot be true. The fact is that they *led* the team within the company that actually effected the turnaround. As the team leader, it seems, they got much, perhaps most of the credit, particularly in the media, and emerged as heroes, or 'company doctors', another term now popular in the management press. Indeed, we ourselves have set out the role played by 'company doctors' worldwide in our book *Company Rescue: How to Manage a Business Turnaround* (1987), but we make the point that no one person can ever achieve the results that are attributed to him: a team is needed to implement the decisions that are taken.

FORD'S PROJECT TAURUS

The same thinking applies to the turnaround at Ford, symbolised by their Taurus/Sable project. The name of the then chief executive, Philip Caldwell, is often mentioned as the one who inspired the production revolution that took place, but there was also his successor, Don Petersen, and the company's president, Harold Poling. This team of three, and perhaps many more, played a part, each contributing individual skill and personality in order to ensure the success of the project as a whole. Because this was so, the term *Team Taurus* was the term used to describe everyone connected with this particular project. It is Peters (1989), writing under the somewhat unusual title *Thriving on Chaos* who brings us details of the Ford Taurus Project. Ford are known to excel in the area of team product development. They seek to remove the barriers between design, engineering, production, marketing, sales and purchasing. However the Taurus team went far beyond that, whilst creating a car that excelled in design and quality. At the same time, the development cost was only half the normal development cost. This was achieved by maintaining simultaneous action on a number of fronts, instead of adopting the normal sequential process. Let us explain.

In the normal sequential process of car development, the designers create a conceptual design which is then developed by the engineers. The manufacturing and purchasing people then set up the necessary tooling and select the best suppliers on the basis of competitive tendering. Production is then taken in hand and other departments, such as marketing, legal and dealer service become involved. Finally the customer enters the picture. Should there be any hitch in this programme, the problem is referred back to the designers. Of course, the further the project is along this process of development, the more expensive does any change become. Once the tooling has been completed any change becomes very expensive indeed, hence change at this late stage must be avoided.

However, Project Taurus was tackled very differently to this, right from its inception. All the relevant disciplines were brought together as a team and the various steps were taken simultaneously as well as sequentially. The team that was built up included production, sales and marketing people right from the beginning. Even the dealers were consulted at a very early stage, in order to establish what the market needed in a user-friendly car. Insurance companies were consulted on design features that would minimise the effects of accidents and reduce the cost of repairs. Legal and safety advisors gave advice as to likely trends in the law, so that the design would conform right at the start. Here was real teamwork in action, with several multi-disciplinary teams working in tandem.

The production team was providing valuable input long before the car went into production. In the words of Lew Veraldi, the Taurus team project leader:

> We went to all the stamping plants, assembly plants, and put layouts on the walls. We asked them how to make it easier to build. We talked to hourly people ... It's amazing the dedication and commitment you get from people . . . We will never go back to the old ways because we now know so much [about] what they can bring to the party.

A unique procedure was adopted with regard to suppliers. Instead of choosing the lowest tenders, as is usual, the Taurus team identified the suppliers offering the highest quality, and then sought their advice on the development of an economic design, with the understanding that they would be the sole preferred supplier. This had the effect of incorporating such suppliers into the 'team': they became yet another team involved in the project. What is more, these suppliers had a real commitment to the success of the project. Indeed, one supplier, the family-owned company of A O Smith, makers of automotive subframes and the like, went so far as to offer the services of its own draughting department to prepare initial designs for Ford's approval. It will be appreciated that such cooperation provided extremely valuable cross-fertilisation of ideas at the conceptual stage, where changes can be made without much extra cost. Not only was there substantial savings in cost and design time, but major production contracts were being negotiated and set up some three years ahead of production, with the duration of the contract some five years. This also led to cost economies.

Before production started, the customers were afforded a preview of the prototype models and asked to suggest changes. The prototypes were tested and evaluated at length in order to establish any necessary design changes, well before the production assembly started. This was so much better than the traditional method of car production, where the maker waits for customer complaints and then spends a couple of years getting the car right. The Taurus project was very successful, and the key to that success was the close involvement of all concerned, right at the start. The vital success factors can be summed up thus:

- multi-functional involvement;

- simultaneous full-time involvement of key members of staff;

- co-location, all the team members being at the same location;

- effective inter-communication, which cuts costs and time;

- assignment of proper resources for the project, not sharing with others;

- intensive outside involvement, particularly with suppliers, dealers and customers.

As a result of these innovations, the new car development cycle at Ford's – and we gather, at other US car makers – has been cut from some six–seven years to four–five years. But even that is not felt to be good enough. In a famous quotable quote, H Ross Perot, noted for 'calling a spade a spade', said:

It takes five years to develop a new car in this country. Heck, we won World War II in four years.

It seems the Japanese have reduced this development period to some three–four years and are now striving to develop and produce a new model within two years. Their approach to the problem is very simple. They do not ask what 'can be', but assert what 'must be'. Achievement of this seemingly impossible goal must lie in a completely new approach to such projects, with radically different methods of organisation.

THE JAPANESE IN THE UNITED STATES

Let us take a brief look at the operations of the Japanese company Nissan, the world's largest motor manufacturer, in the United States. It is Adair (1986) who takes us inside their largest overseas investment, at Smyrna, Tennessee. There are only 15 Japanese in a total workforce of some 1900. The management is largely American, yet this particular factory has been hailed as one of America's best-run companies. The workforce has been broken down into teams, each taking care of a part of the production. There is no demarcation whatever between jobs, all the team members being able to take on one another's jobs. There is never 'my job': it is always 'our job'. Teams rotate on dull jobs that cannot as yet be done by robots, in order to prevent boredom. There is no clocking in, but the team members gather daily some ten minutes before the start of work to discuss the production, task allocation, problems and grievances.

BUT GENERAL MOTORS FAILS

It seems that not all companies are able to apply the principle of teams to their operations. General Motors employed pilot schemes using teams instead of assembly lines for the building of some parts of vehicles. At first this seemed to succeed, but later experience in the early 1970s proved so disappointing that the General Motors management concluded: 'group experiments may suit some people but not all'. What went wrong? Let us illustrate by taking a specific example.

The General Motors Assembly Division handled Chevrolet vans. Over the years this had become a fairly straightforward product, built on an assembly line. However, as an experiment, four people were trained to build a van in a separate building, with the assistance of an engineer. The average time on the assembly line was 8 manhours per van, but the team initially took 13 to 14 manhours per van. However, continuing experience reduced this to 1-1/2 manhours per van, and the process seemed very competitive – as indeed we would expect. But it was not as simple as that. Some of the team members preferred working on the assembly line, and there had to be considerable juggling with the labour force to put together a team that preferred teamwork. The team concept could have been extended to the entire plant, but the workers did not want it. Why?

It seems that the job on the assembly line was fairly simple, one that lent itself to a style and a rhythm where the person could do the job before him in his own way and at his own pace, without really having to think, or exert himself. But with a team each person has a lot of different things to do, and the entire psychology of the job changes. The individual has to carry much greater responsibility and instead of having to contend with perhaps three work elements, he may well have to deal with some 20 to 30 elements. It seems the employees at General Motors did not like this extra responsibility. There were also practical problems associated with the handling of all the parts required. What were to be the means of bringing some 15,000 parts together at one spot, to allow the van to be built? The chairman of General Motors is reported as summing up the situation with which they were faced as follows:

> I don't ever forsee the end of the assembly line. We may use different approaches to sub-assembly, to break down the job so that it can be done more effectively. But our experience in the plant is this: the greatest difficulty we have with our employees is not because the job is repetitive so much as the fact that we have to change the job, which we frequently do because of product development or new investment.

What are we to make of that? Why is their experience so much at variance with the many examples we have quoted of highly successful teamwork? It may be that with certain types of manufacture there is a critical manpower which is also the optimum, but we suspect that it was the General Motors management that was at fault. They failed to inspire their employees with the concepts of pride, involvement and commitment: it is these factors that are the essence of successful teamwork.

16 Collaboration Across Europe

SUMMARY

We now look at teamwork as applied in some European countries, and particularly the United Kingdom. We are dealing with countries that have a very different industrial background to, say, the United States, and that is reflected in their approach to the development of teams. Having surveyed the use of the team philosophy worldwide, we have now been able to see how the various theories and concepts that we have already set out and will continue to demonstrate in relation to teams and their leaders, work out in practice.

TEAMWORK IN THE CONSTRUCTION INDUSTRY

The construction industry is largely project-based. This means that it offers an ideal opportunity for the demonstration of teamwork and its achievements. Some construction companies recognise the value of teamwork: typical of these is Taylor Woodrow, who have a logo strongly suggestive of teamwork, or cooperative effort. Their logo consists of a number of men pulling on a rope. As if to drive the message home to all their staff, their house magazine is titled 'Team Spirit'. John Laing International is another construction company that places great emphasis on teamwork. John Armitt, the deputy managing director, presented a paper at a British Institute of Management conference in 1985 with the title 'Creating commitment in project based industries'. Commitment is of course the essence of successful teamwork.

Construction is a creative industry, with a permanent, highly functional and very visible result that can be clearly seen. When possible, the families of the workers can tour the site to see what is being achieved. All this induces pride in what is going on. Those working on the site should be able to identify themselves with their group or team, know their foreman, and understand their immediate objective. It is the responsibility of management to ensure that tools and materials are available as required. Many a dispute, and poor productivity, are the result of a failure to follow these simple guidelines.

Teamwork is the very essence of every construction project. No one individual can conceive, design, build and commission a construction project, however small. Such projects demand the skills of many people, all committed and motivated, who have to be brought together at the right place and in the right sequence. Commitment within a team amounts to having a positive answer to the question: 'Are you with us? Is your objective the same as ours?' Of course there have been many projects, even major ones, where the answers to these questions have been in the negative. It is thought that financial reward and economic necessity will urge people on to work, but it doesn't always happen that way.

The Central Electricity Generating Board (CEGB) planned Europe's largest oil-fired power station on the Isle of Grain, and sought to have the plant built economically and on time, but they failed. They could not get the 2000-strong workforce to cooperate and share their desire to meet this goal. The people working on the project received very good money but there was a complete lack of commitment.

THE FALKLAND AIRFIELD PROJECT

As Adair (1986) has pointed out, John Laing have sought to combine personal and company goals. The Falkland Airfield Project is typical of successful Laing projects. To secure this particular contract they formed a consortium with Mowlem International Limited and Amey Roadstone

Construction Limited, know as Laing-Mowlem-ARC, or LMA. The joint-venture board appointed a bid manager, and extensive discussions between the three companies followed, with a free exchange of experience on labour, plant, staffing levels and material resources. Each of the member companies concentrated on a particular aspect of the project, agreed beforehand, and there were weekly meetings to review progress. When the time came to submit their tender, there was a final settlement meeting, which took some two days, with the three chairmen and several senior directors in attendance. The tender preparation team worked until 2.30 am on the day of submission, and everyone seemed committed to winning the project. The successful completion and submission of the tender was in itself a team achievement, and the enthusiasm which is generated in such circumstances can be very infectious and long lasting.

The Falkland Islands are situated some 8000 miles from the home base of these companies, and the construction force had to be completely self-reliant. There were extensive logistics problems, difficult communications and a complete absence of harbour facilities. There is no doubt that a novel proposal in the LMA tender, that of using a ship as a floating jetty head, contributed significantly to the success both of their tender and the project. Figure 16.1 gives a view of the *MV Merchant Providence* anchored firmly offshore for this purpose. There was a Bailey Bridge leading to the shore, which can be clearly seen. A road had to be built from the ship to the site.

With this project, as with all projects, the project manager's main task is to win commitment by setting realistic goals and clear targets. Whilst he has to be a quick decision maker, and some of his decisions may not be popular, he has to lead, and this is done by example. The quality of the food for his workforce should receive just as much attention as the quality of his concrete. He can secure commitment only by commanding respect, and this is secured by maintaining close personal communication with the workforce. There is no doubt that the conduct of the project manager, the team leader, is the key to the success of the project.

Figure 16.1

Construction projects present a special problem in terms of commitment, since there can be no guarantee of permanent employment. Every project comes to an end, and there may or may not be another project, and further employment, to follow. John Armitt, the project manager on the Falkland Islands project was intimately and personally involved in supervising a large UK labour force in the late 1970s, before he came to manage the Falkland Islands project in 1983. There was no incentive scheme on either of these projects, but much attention was paid to explaining in detail to the workforce all that was entailed. The criteria for recruitment were also clearly established right from the beginning, and maintained throughout the project.

With the Falkland Islands project, the essence of the project was meeting deadlines: the airport became operational on time because the project management team adopted an unconventional approach. They were innovative, as demonstrated in particular by the setting up of the bridgehead, the institution of a ferry service to get employees home on leave regularly, and the provision of a ship charter service for the supply of materials. A similar spirit was inspired in the workforce, with the result that a news feature reporting interviews with individual workers on the site quoted them as speaking of the 'fantastic companionship' and saying: 'we're all in this together – we're going to win through together'.

The management philosophy called for decision making throughout the organisation, expressed in the injunction: 'don't make decisions too easily – but *make* them!' The fact that the project manager was on site, despite its remoteness, also contributed to the feeling that they were all one team, with a common purpose. We are sure that to some extent the feeling of team spirit was developed by their relative isolation, but the important thing is that they all operated as a team. Hence their eventual success: a project built on time and within budget.

Laing now hold fairly large staff meetings regularly, when the entire staff in a region get together, and the local director briefs them all about the company's current business, how the company is faring financially, what are the problems, and what the future prospects. This is followed by general questions and open discussion. These meetings have proved very popular and well worthwhile. It is another step in the development of the team spirit, giving the employees a feeling of involvement and responsibility, thereby strengthening their commitment to the company and its objectives. There is no doubt that this is particularly difficult to achieve in the construction industry.

THE BECHTEL STORY

The Bechtel Group are a multinational construction company based in the United States. Our present story is of teamwork in Bechtel Great Britain Limited. The account is given by Garth Ward, one of its project managers, and reported by Adair (1986). The objective was to create effective teams in a project-based industry that operated with the matrix-type organisation typical of the construction industry. With such an organisational framework communication problems can be quite serious, but these problems can be avoided or minimised by the use of task forces, whose members are physically located in one area; ie whilst working under the guidance of their respective departmental heads, they are located with the task force, rather than in their department. This helps to give identity to the team. Whilst with the task force, they are responsible to the project manager running their particular project. Thus every team member has two superiors to whom he must look: the project manager and the manager of his department.

After the project is completed, the individual returns to his department, or perhaps moves to another project. But how is one to develop motivation and team loyalty, when the loyalty of its members is so patently divided? This is achieved by allowing the project manager a very substantial voice in the salary, promotion prospects and future employment of the members of the team. Whilst we are using Bechtel as an example, we should make it clear that this particular management approach is common right across the construction industry.

In a larger sense, team building for a successful project must also bring in the project owner, suppliers, subcontractors, the workforce at the job site and their unions. They all have unique problems, which will require a unique approach. Conflict is possible between the project team at the site and the support staff at the head office of the construction company, due to the very different nature of their work. The site staff have the responsibility of translating the drawings and specifications issued from head office into a physical construction in the field, and this requires the utmost cooperation and understanding between the two major groups, or teams involved.

The position is further complicated by the fact that those at head office are in effect in control of site operations, even though a Site Manager, or a Construction Manager, will have been appointed. This duplication of supervision can easily lead to conflict. It would be far better to keep the two teams completely separate and independent, each with their own objectives. But this is hardly practical. The problem can be resolved to some extent by giving the project manager at the site full executive power, but few companies are prepared to go that far. Yet a proper team spirit has to be developed. Another approach is to introduce the site personnel, including the site project manager to the project at the earliest possible moment, long before the site team is set up. If they are involved at the proposal stage, as indeed they were with the Laing project mentioned earlier, then there is a real opportunity for team spirit to develop.

TURNAROUND AT ICI

ICI is a major chemical manufacturing multinational, with headquarters in the United Kingdom. There was a time when one of ICI's nine divisions was losing £100 million a year, and two others were also substantial loss makers. Five years later the company was making an all-time record profit of some £1 billion, the first British company ever to achieve this enviable distinction. How was this turnaround achieved? It was done by giving top priority to the development of management *leadership* in order to create:

- a clear sense of direction, with hard and effective work;

- a confidence in people's ability to achieve challenging objectives;

- a belief in and identification with the organisation;

- people holding together when the going is rough;

- a respect for and a trust in managers.

Notice in this summary the continuing emphasis on the importance of people and groups, and the implementation of teamwork. The man behind this amazing turnaround was most certainly the company chairman Sir Harvey Jones who describes in his autobiography (1987) the way in which this transformation was achieved.

There were management development courses in-house, the emphasis being placed upon what a manager should do to achieve objectives, pull the team together and develop the individuals in it. The manager, to be a leader, must feel personally responsible for all the members of the team; must set the direction in which the team has to go and accept the responsibilities of leadership; and must state the objectives clearly, keeping the members of the team fully informed. This will encourage commitment, help the team to achieve its objectives and improve the standards of personal performance.

A TRANSNATIONAL PROJECT

A series of articles in the *Financial Times* by Lorenz, one of their regular writers on industrial matters, first drew our attention to the achievements of the Swedish company Electrolux. This success story gives us another outstanding example of the success of the team approach. The story opens with the launch of the company's new highly sophisticated fridge-freezer, called the *Quattro 500*. This unit had a unique feature: several temperature zones to allow for the proper storage of various kinds of food, including fresh chilled products. The organisation evolved for the develop-

ment and marketing of this new fridge-freezer was said by
Lorenz to be impossible: yet it worked! The problem was
that Electrolux had to reconcile the need to decentralise
with the need to coordinate the activities of its several
domestic appliance companies in various countries.

But first the development of the *Quattro 500* itself. This
was a team effort that was nevertheless scattered across a
number of countries. The objective was to develop a fridge-
freezer unit that would be suitable for the company's world
markets, using a multi-disciplinary task force coming from
both Europe and the United States. Indeed, there were
periodic meetings on both sides of the Atlantic during the
development phase of the project. It is interesting to see
what was done where during the various phases of the
design and development work:

-   design in Italy;
-   engineering in Finland, with Swedish assistance;
-   marketing in Britain;
-   production initially in Finland, but later also in the
    United States.

One might well think that this approach was far removed
from teamwork, but it was not so in fact. The project leader
was one Heikki Takanen, a Finn based in Stockholm, appro-
priately nicknamed the company's Mr Cold. He explains
the approach as follows:

> This approach must become a model for the fu-
> ture. We not only want to create common projects
> that span several units, but a process that allows
> responsibilities to be transferred between them as
> projects develop.

It was not easy. Not only was there the problem of communication between nationals with different cultures, but each
country has its own traditions. There was a particularly
interesting problem with the relationship between the
Swedish headquarters and its recently acquired Italian
company Zanussi. Real sensitivity was required to ensure

an effective blend of two very different cultures. What is more, as the strength and independence of the several divisions grew, as was only to be expected – that was the result of the policy of decentralisation – some of the head office staff in Sweden began to press for more central authority. Nevertheless the process of change continued.

One product line manager, Leif Johansson, talking about what are called the 'white goods' (refrigerators, freezers and the like) and the company structure, still in development as he spoke, saw it all as very much a process of trial and error. The company had to adjust to a changing environment and internal conflicts. According to him – and he was right – people were far more important than the company structure, a view central to our present theme:

> [it is] a quite impossible organisation, but the only one that works . . . if you ask me who takes the decisions, it's not all that clear . . . the organisation only works provided the people involved want it to.

This is yet another view of the way in which teams should operate. During its rapid growth in the 1980s, Electrolux created some 500 small business units within each product line, the nationally-based companies being the profit centre. The company has managed to strike a very difficult but fine balance between the various possible approaches to decentralisation and team development. The problem was the more complicated because the company was a multinational, with very significant manufacturing groups in a number of countries. There was also the problem of coping with such diverse businesses as aluminium manufacture and commercial cleaning services. What has emerged is the coveted matrix-type structure, though it still has in-built conflicts.

To cope with these problems Johansson has formed a new forum, called the '1992 Group'. This consists of managers from the several countries who are required to oversee the development of all aspects of product line strategy in their regions and develop an international perspective. Johansson is reluctant to go all the way, and establish an international management. He has no desire to abolish the position of regional authority now occupied by the managers in the several countries. We would have thought that in any event it was a good policy to develop the team spirit, which is very readily built into national groups. If the leader comes from outside it is unlikely to be so effective. This 'nationalistic' approach has been encouraged by the experience of other multinationals. Conflict seems inevitable between countries, but there is no point in seeking to subdue it. Better to let it surface, and allow top management to resolve the problems it brings. But all in all we have here yet another example of successful teamwork.

17 Case Studies in Teamwork Worldwide

SUMMARY

Having looked at outstanding examples of successful teamwork in the United States and Europe, we now consider some case histories from other countries and continents. There is no doubt that Japan offers us many outstanding examples of successful teamwork, but we have brought forward various examples of their teamwork in other chapters, so have confined ourselves here to just one detailed case study from that country. We also bring you some remarkable case studies from other countries, such as Australia, India, Indonesia, Papua New Guinea and South Africa. Each case study brings its own lessons, but the abiding theme is: success through teamwork.

THE EXAMPLE OF JAPAN

Japanese managers are essentially team builders and it is through this approach to management that Japanese companies have been so successful over the years. Their basic philosophy is that team objectives should be ambitious, but attainable. Maude (1978) outlines a number of other characteristics displayed by Japanese teams:

- they are ambitious and have clear objectives;

- each member understands clearly his role and his responsibilities;

- all team members share the same values and goals;

- there is frank, candid and continuous two-way communication;

- the team members have diverse skills and experience;

- grievances are sorted out, giving a high morale and low staff turnover;

- the leader constantly stresses the successful completion of the task.

Japan, more than any other country, has minimised the gap in salary and perquisites between the chief executive and those who work on the shop floor. This has been a major help in inculcating the team spirit, with its consequent high staff morale and ever-increasing productivity. Even in the United States, where it might be thought that other standards would prevail, the chief executive of the Nissan plant at Smyrna, Tennessee wears the company issue overalls at work, even when important visitors are being received. Peters and Austin (1985) make the point that this has an almost magical effect on the workforce. Actions speak louder than words, and this uniformity in dress declares unequivocally that they are all part of the same team. Such a thing as uniform clothing may seem a small thing, but it means a lot to the average worker on the shop floor and ensures that they work with enthusiasm and recognise that they have common cause with the management.

Honda is a Japanese company known worldwide, first for its motorbikes and more recently for its cars. Attention has been drawn to the company's lavish spending on research and development, and the role that technological advancement was playing in Honda's success. But the president of the company, whilst admitting that Honda was indeed technically in advance of its rivals, maintained that this alone was not enough to bring success. Far more important, in his view, were quality and productivity, factors which depend both on the performance of the workers and on the quality of the management.

The rigid organisational structure present in many companies is not conducive to success, and this is most certainly absent at the Honda works. There is no clear-cut organisation or company chart for Honda, but the company *does* use the project team concept.

Just to illustrate the motivation that can exist in a properly inspired and led workforce, the story is told of the Honda worker who, returning home from work each evening, never failed to straighten up the windshield wipers of every Honda car that he passed! With such strong feeling of loyalty, the workers will inevitably be continuously striving for ever higher quality. How to instil such loyalty and devotion to duty is another matter. The singular success of the Japanese is due not to complex management systems, but to their attaching proper importance to their most vital resource: those actually working on the project.

RISE OF THE ROBOT

The Robot Institute of America defines a robot, *inter alia*, as 'a programmable, multi-function manipulator designed to move material, parts, tools or specialised devices through variable programmed motions for the performance of a variety of tasks'. On the other hand, the Japanese Industrial Robot Association (JIRA) feels that a robot cannot be defined. Humphreys (1985) tells us that in 1961 three industrial robots were sold worldwide – two to General Motors and one to the Ford Motor Company. This particular development started in the United States, now totally outdistanced by Japan, as has occurred in many a field.

The assessment of the number of robots now operating in Japan and elsewhere varies from source to source, but it seems to be generally agreed that whereas the number of robots in operation in the United States in 1983 was some 15,000, in Japan it was said to be twice as many. In addition, many of the robots now operating in the United States were actually made in Japan.

How has this dramatic advance in Japan been accomplished? We believe that the successful project is above all the result of close teamwork, and for this the team members must be motivated. We would like to coin the phrase: 'motivation is the means – success is the end'.

Japanese managers are essentially team builders. They lead rather than manage, and do this by a process of consensus. This is so much better than passing down instructions without discussion. There is therefore free and honest communication up and down the management structure, and this creates a healthy family relationship, with its warm, cooperative atmosphere and strong team spirit. Physical factors also contribute to this concept. Open-plan offices not only demonstrate that there are no barriers, but they encourage the interchange of ideas and information between junior and senior colleagues.

The Japanese have for years practised the use of the task force and the project team to resolve specific problems and to accomplish specific tasks. The development of robotics is an outstanding example, in that the cooperation was not only within companies, but between companies and with the relevant government organisations. Key personnel were taken from the various companies interested in developing robots, and project teams were set up for development research, but once the work was completed they went back to their own companies. Byrne (1983) tells us that a pioneer Japanese company in the field of robotics was Kawasaki, who bought the technology back in 1968 from the US company Unimation. But the government also became deeply involved, committing some US$35 million to robot research. The end result is that Japan now dominates in robotics.

The project team approach and the task force concept are ingrained in Japanese culture and are now a completely natural way of working. Unlike their Western counterparts, Japanese companies rarely have a formal organisation chart, and the all-important managing director does not even appear on such charts as are drawn up. Many deputies who have purely line functions are also not mentioned, despite their key importance in company operations. Even a highly successful company such as Honda is not at all clear as to its organisational structure.

DIAGNOSE AND CURE

Turning round a failing company is always more challenging for management than maintaining an on-going company. Sometimes it is easier for an outside management team to diagnose what is going on, although a competent in-house management team can sense the mistakes that are being made and do something about it. Belbin (1984) was called in as a consultant by Simpson Limited of Adelaide, Australia. This company became interested in team building, having itself diagnosed that this was the problem area. So its managers were put through a training programme including the 'Teamopoly' exercise, a management game devised by Belbin.

The Simpson group operates in the consumer durables field, being particularly known in Australia for its washing machines, clothes dryers and cookers. What was the cause of the trouble? Hitherto a highly protected market, Australia was gradually lifting and reducing its import tariffs, and this had an adverse influence on the local manufacturers producing for their home market.With the Simpson group, the danger was met by bringing in a new chief executive, but his policies were too revolutionary. Too many changes were made in senior management and this had a demoralising effect. Belbin advised a change in the approach. So the senior management were given a strong feeling that they were wanted and open management practices were brought in to encourage team working. Each product group was put in charge of a multi-disciplinary team, and outstanding personal development in individuals was spotted, encouraged and rewarded. Test results at top management level showed that whilst there was in general a shift to the classic mixed team approach to management, some of the new executives, though of high ability, were found to be lacking in team spirit. This was highlighted during the 'Teamopoly' exercise, which demonstrated that these particular executives were working as 'loners' and thus threatening the teamwork policy. Once this had been diagnosed, a training programme was instituted to change attitudes.

SUCCESS IN THE PUBLIC SECTOR

Bureaucratic management, as is common in government organisations, has a very poor reputation. Hence it is blamed for the failure of manufacturing operations in the public sector: there are examples from almost every country in the world. Yet the dead hand of bureaucracy can be overcome, and the Kudremukh iron ore project, in southern India, is an outstanding example. This is one of the largest mining and beneficiation projects in the world. It was developed in difficult, hilly terrain under the most severe climatic conditions. In that area the heavy monsoon rains last for some four months, and for most of the year there are strong winds and much fog. Indeed, it is said that the Bhadra river valley, where the Kudremukh community is situated, has the unwelcome distinction of being the third wettest place known on earth. In the monsoon season the average rainfall is some 6000mm. In 1980, the year in which the Kudremukh plant was started up, the rainfall was exceptional even by local standards, exceeding 9500mm, with 417mm (17 in) in one 24-hour period, yet another record. But, thanks to proper project planning this US$650 million venture, with a capacity of 7 million tonnes per year of iron ore pellets, was successfully completed to a very tight construction schedule: only 40 months were allowed to mechanical completion. The basic reasons for this were said to be teamwork *par excellence*, which was translated into:

- carrying out detailed design and construction simultaneously;
- undertaking a number of independent activities in parallel;
- delivering equipment to site whenever possible fully or partially assembled;
- the full use of standardisation and modular design.

Mirchandani (1983) makes the point that the pragmatic and flexible policy adopted by the Indian government also helped substantially towards the successful completion of this particular project.

The Kudremukh Project Office was set up in November 1975. A small project team was brought together, with personnel from MECON (Metallurgical & Engineering Consultants (India) Limited), HSCL (Hindustan Steelworks Construction Limited) and SAIL (Steel Authority of India Limited). These were all public sector organisations. Then there was the operating company KIOCL (Kudremukh Iron Ore Company Limited) and MET-CHEM (Canadian MET-CHEM Consultants), the mining associate and engineering constructor called in from overseas to assist.

So the principle of teamwork was established, with individuals nominated from their several companies to form some three teams – the government advisory team, the operating company team and the overseas consultant's team – to develop the project and bring it to fruition. A total of some 80 contracts were let for civil and structural work both at Kudremukh and at Mangalore, the port from which the iron ore pellets were to be shipped abroad. At peak, in October 1979, MET-CHEM had a total of 40 expatriates supervising the construction, supported by some 400 Indian personnel at site. There were also a number of outside agencies employed for surveying, quality control and similar work. Considering the difficult terrain, the harsh climate and the inaccessibility of the site, completion within the time schedule established was a real challenge. But that challenge was met and overcome.

As with any major project, there were serious problems to be encountered and overcome, and it is here that teamwork comes into its own. Decisions have to be made forthwith, if the situation is to be saved. Some of the equipment came from Calcutta, but floods delayed delivery. Other equipment came from Canada, and delivery was threatened by a dock strike in North America, necessitating the diversion of the equipment to other ports not affected by the strike. Then one Indian manufacturer had serious labour problems and was on the point of failure. This situation was only redeemed by the transfer of the unfinished equipment to another fabricator overnight under a stay order from the Madras High Court. Despite these setbacks, the plant was completed on time *and within budget*, the several emergencies being handled with decisive, resolute and immediate action. There is no doubt that this project has been an outstanding success, and *Business India* attributes much of this success to the project direction given by the dynamic chairman and managing director, Mr K C Khanna. He inspired his teams to commit themselves wholeheartedly to what he saw as a national cause. Expectations were high, but they were met!

MULTINATIONAL TEAMS AT WORK

Our next case study relates to projects in Indonesia, and involves technology transfer in relation to fertiliser plants to that country. Indonesia is the fourth most densely populated country in the world, and it also has the world's largest archipelago, with some 13,000 islands. These include Java, Sumatra, Bali and most of Borneo, now known as Kalimantan. We shall be looking at a hydroelectric power plant and aluminium smelter, built at Asahan on the island of Sumatra, and a series of fertiliser manufacturing plants built on that island and on Java.

The government of Indonesia has continually striven to develop its own natural resources and also to ensure that it will ultimately be self-sufficient not only in terms of food and energy, but also in relation to the design and operation of the plants it needs. This demands continuous and intensive technology transfer, with the training of large numbers of people. An American firm, M W Kellogg, has been closely involved in this process of technology transfer in Indonesia since 1971, the year in which self-sufficiency in fertiliser production became a national objective. To achieve this objective, a new Indonesian engineering and construction management company was set up at Jakarta, P T Kellogg Sriwidjaja (KELSRI), as a joint venture between the Indonesian government and M W Kellogg.

Meanwhile, by 1978 M W Kellogg had completed its fourth large-scale ammonia-urea plant complex in Indonesia. Built for P T Pupuk at Kujang near Dauwan in central

West Java, the complex utilises natural gas feedstock provided by the national oil company Pertimina. Not only this plant, but the previous three plants had all been completed well to time and within budget, as shown in Table 17.1.

	Months to Completion		Project Cost	
	Target	Actual	Target m.US$	Actual m.US$
PUSRI II	30	34	67	77
PUSRI III	32	31	166	165
PUSRI IV	30	26	157	130

Table 17.1

There is no doubt that the success of the PUSRI projects has been due to teamwork, with complete cooperation on terms of equality between the owner, a nationalised company, and the contractor, who had come from overseas. The various plants are said to be working very well indeed, completely under local control. Indeed, it was reported that in 1983 Indonesia set a world record in urea fertiliser output with over 100 per cent capacity utilisation with some if its plants: this is most difficult to achieve.

The knowledge brought to the country from abroad has been avidly assimilated and applied. This attitude is crucial to teamwork. There must be a willingness to listen and learn, and this attitude of mind must begin right at the top, with the chief executive. What is more, we are *never* too old to learn.

The Asahan project is different only in that it demonstrates cooperation between Indonesia and Japan, rather than between Indonesia and the United States. The completion of this major project, accomplished with the full cooperation of the Japanese government, was the realisation of a

long-cherished dream for Indonesia. It has special significance in terms of cooperation, for as President Soeharto of
Indonesia stated:

> The completion of the Asahan project means that
> the dream has become a reality through coopera-
> tion between Japan and Indonesia. This successful
> cooperation not only has great economic signific-
> ance, but is also a sign of a monumental friend-
> ship, which will always be remembered from
> generation to generation.

The project as now built comprises two power stations, a
120 km transmission line and a 3-line aluminium smelter. In
addition, a very substantial infrastructure had to be developed, including roads, water supply, communication facilities, houses and schools. Both parties, Indonesia and Japan,
had a substantial interest in the successful completion of the
project. Japan benefited because it secured a cheap source of
supply of aluminium, whilst Indonesia benefited from the
social and economic development of North Sumatra that
resulted.

This mutual interest was brought right through to the
project teams involved in the project, so that enthusiasm
and commitment pervaded every member of the project
teams. The project manager should recognise the powerful
influence for good that such personal involvement brings,
and should therefore take continuing and positive steps to
inform the workforce as to the ultimate aims and benefits of
the project on which they are engaged.

INNOVATIVE SPIRIT MOVES MOUNTAINS

Now we go to Papua New Guinea and a most challenging
project. Pintz (1984) has described this project in great
detail. The Ok Tedi Gold and Copper Project ('ok' means
river in Papuan and the river Tedi ran adjacent to the project
site), costing some US$2.5 billion, involved the mining,
processing and shipping of more than a billion tonnes of
copper ore that had been found beneath an isolated mountain top in north-west Papua New Guinea. What is more,

the copper deposit lay under more than two million troy ounces of high-grade gold ore, that naturally enough was to be mined first, yielding some million troy ounces of gold bullion. All this ore was located on the top of a mountain in the middle of a rain forest near the Equator. It is said to be one of the wettest places on earth, with some 8 metres (311 inches) of rain falling annually. The ground is unstable and landslides commonplace. The whole area is covered by nearly impenetrable forest.

The materials and supplies for the project, which came from all over the world, entered Papua New Guinea at Port Moresby. There they were transferred to barges and shipped some 500 km across the gulf to the mouth of the Fly River, and then a further 800 km up that river to the town of Kianga. Then there was a further 160 km to go, up the steep mountain road which led to the project site. This road had to be specially built as part of the project, and carved out of the forest. Not only did the project team have to contend with the site conditions, but also with the labour force employed on the project. Some of the local people employed on the project had never seen a wheel until twenty years ago; much less had they sat in the cab of an enormous bulldozer. Thus there had to be an intensive training effort, first in the classroom and then on the job. Yet, despite the high proportion of 'green' staff, the accident rate was kept to a minimum: less than that normally encountered on construction sites in the United States.

This was a project demanding an innovative spirit from all concerned, especially those in effect isolated from the world at the project site. That such an innovative spirit, so crucial to effective teamwork, prevailed, is well illustrated by some comments on the project by the main contractor's project manager:

> This was a project that you like to tell people you worked on. It was a mega-project, a one-of-its-kind challenge, something that provided much more than just a new mining project. There's a tremendous amount of satisfaction when you

Figure 17.1

complete something that seems so difficult. It's just a hell-of-a-good feeling for all of us to see this job come together knowing what we accomplished to get it there.

INTERNATIONAL TEAMWORK

We have presented case studies from various continents, that demonstrate the need for effective teamwork not only within the company, but also across the nation and even across national frontiers. A case study from South Africa is outstanding in the way in which companies from several different continents were able to team up and so complete what has been called the Sasol Project. The name 'Sasol' stands for *South African Coal, Oil and Gas Company* when that company name is written in Afrikaans, the Dutch-related language of the Republic of South Africa. The plant – in effect two plants, Sasol II and Sasol III – was built to produce liquid fuels, including petrol, from coal, which South Africa has in abundance. Sasol I came on stream back in 1954, and Sasol II was started in 1975. The Fluor Corporation, of Irvine, California, was appointed as managing contractor and the plant was to be located at Secunda, some 150 km east of Johannesburg in the Eastern Transvaal. The plant, together with Sasol III, occupies a total area of some 15 square kilometres (15,000 hectares). The aerial photograph presented as Figure 17.1 gives a vivid impression of the size of the complex. The scope of the involvement of international companies other than Fluor is demonstrated by the following list of the major overseas engineering contractors employed to supply specialist equipment and services:

Badger, Cambridge, Massachusetts, USA

Deutsche Babcock, Oberhausen, West Germany

Fluor Mining & Metals, Redwood City, Ca, USA

L'Air Liquide, Champigny, France

Linde, Munich, West Germany

Lurgi, Frankfurt-am-Main, West Germany

Mobil, New York, USA

Universal Oil Products (UOP), Des Plaines, Ill, USA

So successful were these contractors in completing Sasol II on time and within budget, that the contracts for Sasol III were being awarded to them even before Sasol II had been completed and commissioned. This indicates a high degree of confidence both in the process and the contractors who had been building Sasol II.

Sasol III was to be largely a 'chinese copy' of Sasol II, using the existing drawings and the temporary facilities already available. With two projects now being handled effectively as one, there were further economies in both cost and time. As a result, Sasol III came on stream very quickly after Sasol II, early in 1982.

The total investment in the two projects was of the order of US$6.5 billion, taking the US dollar as equivalent to 1.15 Rand, as it was then. Thus far the project. How was it managed?

The construction site was divided into six zones, each zone in turn being subdivided into areas. This resulted in a total, for Sasol II, of more than sixty construction areas, each of which was handled entirely separately, with its own project team, critical path network and the like. Similarly, of course, for Sasol III. So all in all there were in effect some 120 separate projects, each handled autonomously, with its own project team.

It is very evident from the ultimate success of the project that this system of project management was very effective, and once again we have demonstrated the value of setting up small teams. We have said that the optimum number of personnel for such teams is of the order of ten, and this seems to be proven in practice. Larger teams are by no means so effective. But in the case of the Sasol Project, we not only have effective teamwork on site, but we have teamwork across continents, with companies speaking different languages all cooperating together. This is teamwork at its best!

Part 6

PARTICIPATION IS THE ANSWER

18 The Significance of Quality

SUMMARY

The maintenance of high standards in relation to quality is seen to be essential to success. This has been found to be cost effective, and the supreme exponent of the art has been Japanese industry. We therefore take a close look at the way in which the Japanese have achieved what is called 'total quality control'. In part this is due to 'quality circles', which brings us back to the concept of the team and its effective utilisation. The achievement of total quality control is seen to be the responsibility of management and, above all, senior management. Management will strive after total quality control once it has been demonstrated that it has a substantial payoff. Complete management commitment to quality control is a must if it is to be successful: this calls for the quality concept to be incorporated in the company mission and culture.

INTRODUCTION

Quality seems these days to have become the clue to success in whatever field one looks. It all began some thirty years ago now when quality was seen to be the root to what has been called the Japanese 'miracle'. High quality, it seems, sold Japanese products worldwide. A great deal has been written about the significance of quality and the way to achieve a quality product, but we make no apology for writing about this subject, specially since it is directly related to teamwork and team effort. At the heart of every achievement of high quality lies a tremendous team effort, and we devote an entire chapter (Chapter 20) to quality circles.

241

Whilst the attainment and maintenance of quality in production was originally a Western concept, it seems that the Japanese were the first to take it to heart and incorporate it fully into their culture, both social and business. Quality was assumed to cost money, but the Japanese disposed of this myth, demonstrating that in fact quality *saved* money. The proper maintenance of quality in production is so cost effective that, with the same facilities, a larger volume of goods can be produced than was produced before – and all of high quality, thus shattering another myth. In other words, the proper maintenance of quality in production leads to increased profits. This may seem an obvious statement today, accepted worldwide, but it was originally a revolutionary concept.

TOTAL QUALITY CONTROL

How is quality achieved and maintained? Let us return to the Japanese for a lesson. Masao Nemoto (1987) wrote a book on total quality control for management which has been translated from the Japanese by David Lu. Masao Nemoto joined Toyota Motors soon after his graduation from the Tokyo Institute of Technology in 1943. He finally rose to be that company's managing director in 1976. Since 1982 he has been president of Toyoda Gosei, who are a supplier of major parts to Toyota Motors. Toyoda Gosei received the Demming Application Prize in 1985, after Masao Nemoto introduced the 'total quality control' concept to that company.

David Lu, the translator and editor of Nemoto's book, is himself the author of some ten books, and is well equipped for the job, having earlier translated Kaoru Ishikawa's classic, *What is Quality Control?* Masao Nemoto's book may well be considered an appropriate sequel to that earlier title. His book carries an introduction in the form of a Foreword, written by Shoichiro Toyoda, the current president of Toyota Motors, together with some author's notes relating to the English edition and an introduction by David Lu. Shoichiro Toyoda speaks of Masao Nemoto in glowing terms. The phenomenal commercial success of Toyota

Motors and its affiliates is credited largely to Masao Nemoto's 'total quality control' programme, associated with his personal ability as an administrator, manager and educator. Even Toyota car dealers were found to display an interest in quality control, and Masao Nemoto spent his weekends expounding its principles to them.

The book he eventually wrote, together with the English translation, was prompted by the Japanese Union of Scientists and Engineers (JUSE). David Lu, during a tour of Toyoda Gosei conducted by Masao Nemoto, was amazed by the casual and informal way in which workers asked Masao Nemoto questions and got an instant reply. Thus David Lu witnessed 'a master at work in his own speciality – that of managing a company, and doing it well'. It seems that Masao Nemoto has a homespun wisdom based on pragmatism, has a warm personality and never scolds his personnel. This has won him both respect and affection. The consequent influence on the working atmosphere is very apparent: an influence which is displayed very effectively in his book. We have to recognise that as the quality of the working life increases, so does productivity: the two are very closely and positively related.

Masao Nemoto's book uses simple language and presents us with a down-to-earth treatment of the vital subject of total quality control. The proven and practical techniques described here can help to increase both efficiency and productivity. What strikes us is the simple methods adopted to improve communication between the specialists and those who have to carry out their ideas: this of course is at the heart of effective teamwork. It seems that a suggestion scheme, properly implemented, can bring a host of money-saving ideas. Proper coordination between the various divisions of the company, another aspect of effective teamwork, is seen to be crucial to success.

Then there are well-designed educational programmes that develop the individual worker's ability to rectify defects. A system for the encouragement of participants to speak at quality circle meetings ensures their effectiveness.

We revert to quality circles in much greater detail in Chapter 20, but for the moment consider the overall benefits of total quality control (according to Nemoto):

- costs, both direct and indirect, are reduced considerably;

- annual policies and goals are readily established;

- priorities are readily set;

- there is 100 per cent defect-free production, thus no repair work or reworking;

- job rotation is easy;

- efficiency can be maintained and waste eliminated.

QUALITY CONTROL THE JAPANESE WAY

Kaoru Ishikawa, already mentioned, is the father of the quality control concept (sometimes called 'total quality control', or 'company wide quality control'). It is the concept that the way people are handled, encouraged and motivated is crucial, which is at the heart of Kaoru Ishikawa's book.

Ishikawa was a graduate in applied chemistry, and he discovered early the importance of statistical methods in relation to the teaching of engineering. He has been, as it were, a missionary in relation to quality control since 1949. The history of quality control and Kaoru Ishikawa's life are inseparable. Japanese management has succeeded in harnesssing the energy of its people more effectively than anyone else and this seems to be largely due to the development of quality circles. In such circles workers interact with their foremen and engineers, all of them working together as a team. This results in problem solving at the workplace, in a calm, relaxed atmosphere, but with a concrete, serious objective in view – the improvement and maintenance of quality.

Whilst the quality circle may be seen as initially an American invention, it was the Japanese who took the concept to heart and developed it extensively throughout their industry. Now, of course, the concept is recognised to be of universal application and is being applied worldwide. Apart from assuring quality, total quality control ensures:

- 100 per cent defect-free production;
- radically improved communications within the company;
- the design and manufacture of products better suited to the customer's requirements;
- detection of false data in relation to production or sales.

It will be appreciated that the above points are very similar to those already made earlier, when we were considering the work of Masao Nemoto, but that of course is only to be expected.

Quality control just cannot thrive if there is labour unrest, with continual dissension, such as is created by the adoption of Theory X, as first postulated by Taylor. The Theory X approach is dehumanising not only for the workers but also for those who oversee them. Management needs to be self-critical, and Kaoru Ishikawa maintains that much of the responsibility for mistakes rests with management: not the worker. Quality control amounted to a revolution in thinking in this context, and it can have many by-products. Kaoru Ishikawa expects that as a result of quality control not only will materials and energy be saved, but that people all over the world will be happier, and the world prosperous and peaceful.

The principles of mutual cooperation exemplified by quality control are applicable not only to corporate organisations but to one's personal life as well: it is a principle of universal application. It is a very practical discipline which recognises and utilises the fundamental attributes of human nature. The principle of teamwork underlying quality control could indeed be the salvation of the world, if it were to be universally applied, but we are far removed from that – yet!

PROJECT TEAMS

WHOSE RESPONSIBILITY IS QUALITY MANAGEMENT?

Don Vaughn, president of M W Kellogg, one of the largest process plant contractors in the world, recognises the responsibility that his company has for quality control, even in a service type industry:

> We're living in a competitive world where quality is not simply a choice – it's a survival issue – at both the corporate and personal level . . . Our quality mission: we will provide advanced technologies, facilities and services which fully satisfy our client's needs and provide greater benefit than those of our competition . . . we want to be first in the industry in quality, value, productivity and cost effectiveness.

Vaughn defines quality in his context as 'doing the right things at the right time' and also to 'do it right the first time'. This is possible only by properly integrating quality management into the company culture. It will not come on its own. Most of the literature dealing with the subject of quality relates to the manufacturing sector, but we have found one writer who deals with the service industry, the type of business with which M W Kellogg are involved. It seems that training about quality management is not enough: a complete change of attitude and habits within the company is essential. This must come from the 'top down', starting with the president himself and imbuing the whole company. Every individual within the company must be 'quality conscious'. Such a change cannot be accomplished overnight but it can be achieved with sustained effort over a period.

Irving (1986), in an interesting and very practical article dealing with quality welding, has a very pertinent comment:

> We have the tools needed to make welding a quality process. The funny thing is that the most appropriate tools walk around on two legs and wear white collars.

Man, not the machine, is the crucial element in determining quality, and it is so often the case that the right men are doing the wrong job, or *vice versa*. It must be an axiom that most of the problems relating to quality are caused by management, not the people who actually do the work. In matters of quality, as with productivity, all too often the worker on the shop floor gets all the blame, when it is no fault of his. Perhaps the real culprit is the pyramidal style of management.

QUALITY IMPROVEMENT – RETURN ON INVESTMENT

A good businessman needs justification before he will incur extra costs. Does improvement in quality bring a payoff? Feigenbaum (1987) wrote an excellent article on this aspect of quality control, and said in that context:

> Quality leveraged companies are likely to have a five-cents-on-the-sales-dollar advantage over their competitors . . . the more successful a product becomes the higher the quality levels it must achieve . . . Quality and costs are a *sum*, not a *difference*: partners, not adversaries.

During the sixties and seventies, the mass production wave in the United States was based on the premise that making products more quickly and more cheaply was the key to success. High quality was not thought to be important. But in the eighties – in the face of intense competition from Japan, other countries in the Far East, and European suppliers, whose products sold primarily on quality – it was realised that, though making products more quickly and more cheaply was essential if one was to be competitive, this was not enough. The products had also to be of high quality. This presented many companies in the West with a daunting task: they had to progress beyond the 'make it quicker and cheaper' situation to one where they also 'made it better'.

As a result, there has been a tremendous change in attitudes. Quality is now seen to be crucial to the success of an enterprise. Thus, in the matter of purchasing, eight out of ten buyers now consider quality to be at least as important, if not more important, than price. Only four out of ten thought that way only ten years ago. The statement 'we'll fix it for you' is now outmoded. The buyer wants a fault-free product: not a product that may fail and require repair. It has also been found that this approach pays off, not only in the short term but also over long periods of time.

A company steadily builds up a reputation for faultless workmanship. Three fundamental principles should be emphasised:

- Quality is what the customer perceives. It is also a moving target and quality improvement must be a continuous and never-ending process. If production volume is increased without ensuring that quality is also improved, then the product is doomed.

- Quality is as important in the service industries as in the manufacturing industries. Just one error in an invoice has been found to create more ill-will than the need to return three or four items because of faults.

- There is no question of a tradeoff between quality and cost. They are a *sum*, not a *difference*; they are partners, not adversaries. Good quality implies a sound and economic use of resources. That quality is costly is a myth.

So what is the return on investment, when better quality is striven for? It is actually much better than any calculation is likely to show, since the intangible benefits far outweigh the tangible benefits. Tallon (1987) makes the point that good quality is by far the best way to keep a customer.

QUALITY WITHOUT TEARS

Let us bring our consideration of the significance of quality to an end by assessing the importance of the role of management. Philip Crosby (1985) has written a book with the title *Quality Without Tears*, which has the subtitle: 'The art of hassle-free management'. The author is certainly well qualified to write on this particular subject, having started his career as a line inspector and ending up some thirty years later as a corporate vice-president of ITT, responsible for quality control worldwide. The subject of quality seems to be his life. Crosby has been in demand by many companies – which has led him to set up as a private consultant. His book shows how, as a management consultant, he has helped hundreds of companies achieve quality quietly and without fuss.

Crosby realised that poor management is the clear cause of most problems, including those of quality, and insists that management commitment is a 'must' if a quality programme is to be implemented and sustained. His approach is exemplified by such statements as:

- management denies that it is the cause of the problem;

- senior management is fully responsible for quality problems;

- quality improvement is a process, not a programme;

- quality has to be defined in accordance with the requirements;

- the system for causing quality is prevention, not appraisal;

- I have never met anyone who was against quality or for hassle.

The main ingredients for an improvement in quality are measurement, determination and education. Quality can indeed be measured in cold, hard, financial terms which are quite convincing. The cost of poor quality is very high: some 25 per cent of operating costs in many manufacturing companies and often as much as 40 per cent in service companies. All this expense can be completely avoided by spending just a few per cent on the preventive and educational actions necessary to achieve high quality. However, if management is not determined enough, or is not committed to quality, then getting it right first time is extremely difficult. To produce zero-defect products and services on time is a concept that must originate with top management. This requires not only commitment, but close control by management at every stage. The important point is that quality can be translated directly into profits: this is the language that management understands and will respond to.

Let us conclude with a quotation from Harold S Geneen, one of the most notable of chief executives, since it sums up the matter. Crosby dedicated his book, *Quality is Free*, to Harold Geneen, and quotes him as follows:

> Quality is not only right, it is free. And it is not only free, it is the most profitable product line we have.

If only management will appreciate this fundamental fact, and realise that whilst quality is not a gift, but something that has to be worked on and developed, it is nevertheless free. Essentially it is management attitudes that make all the difference. Hopefully, these attitudes will change once it is widely realised that quality is a profit maker, not a cost centre.

19 The Role of Productivity

SUMMARY

*Quality and productivity **must** go hand in hand. It is of no use producing a superb quality product unless it can also be produced in a reasonable time at a competitive price. This demands high productivity. So we now look at the relationship that exists – or should exist – between quality and productivity. One common factor is that both depend on people: their active participation and their development into well-knit teams. This involves both the motivation and the morale of the teams: these must always be maintained at a high level. Using practical examples we demonstrate how this can be done.*

QUALITY IS AN ATTITUDE OF MIND

Quality is usually presented as calling for a set of techniques, best developed in what are called 'quality circles'. This is unfortunate and in fact completely erroneous. In fact, Peters and Austin (1985), in writing of excellence and the role played by the leadership in achieving excellence, have a short chapter headed 'Quality is not a technique'. They make the point that, in effect, their entire book is about quality. Why is this? Because quality is *not* a technique. Rather, quality is about care, people, passion, consistency. Quality does not derive from techniques, although of course they play a part. Quality comes from people, their personal care and commitment. It comes from a belief that anything can be made better if you try hard enough, and keep on trying.

251

Quality also comes from people working together in a team with a common purpose. It has to be an obsession: it must form a 100 per cent objective whilst at work: even 99 per cent is just not good enough. That may sound an impossibility, but it isn't. It all depends upon commitment. Edwards Deming, the father of statistical quality control, introduced this concept to the Japanese. He stresses that quality is primarily a function of human commitment. Addressing college students at Utah State University, he made the point thus:

> If you run a company on figures alone you will go under . . . because the most important figures are not there: they are unknown or unknowable. People all over the world think that it is the factory worker that causes problems. He is not your problem . . . he is not allowed to do [a good job] because the management wants figures, more product, and never mind the quality. They measure only in figures . . .

The value of people cannot be assessed financially and put into the company accounts. Yet it is people who govern quality, and it is quality that matters. Let the figures come later, and they should never be allowed to dominate. Perhaps a couple of examples will make the point:

-   McDonald's Ray Kroe visited a franchise of his at Winnipeg, found a single fly, and cancelled the franchise.

-   IBM insist on excellence in *all* that they do. An error in an internal memo is inconsistent with perfection.

But how can one make the maintenance of quality at all times an attitude of mind? Management must of course measure quality, but they must not stop there. They must celebrate high quality and reward it. Then everybody involved will become infected with the desire to maintain quality at all costs, knowing full well that in the long run the cost of quality is actually negative. This question of quality being an attitude of mind was once highlighted by the magazine *Quality: America's Guide to Excellence*. It said:

> We have to grant quality its moral dimension . . .
> It should be recognized as a virtue – something to
> be sought for its own sake – not just a profitable
> strategy. To the Swiss, with their passion for grace
> and precision in everything from pocket knives to
> highway bridges, quality is second nature. Can
> we import not just Swiss products but the atti-
> tudes behind them?

The Americans are posing this question to themselves, but
surely it is a question we should all pose to ourselves.

QUALITY AND PRODUCTIVITY HAND-IN-HAND

There is no doubt that if quality and productivity go hand
in hand, the end result will be a profit. Both quality and
productivity are most difficult to measure in absolute terms.
Indeed, the only ultimate measure of their effectiveness is
the fact that the company makes a good profit. Underlying
good quality and productivity are people, their effectiveness in working together as a team, and the morale that is
maintained in the team.

It is easy enough to say that everyone in the company
should eat, sleep and breathe quality, but how can this be
achieved? There has to be a working procedure, with the
customer defining the quality required.

Let us turn to an example. A detailed analysis of the
American company TRW, said to be a microcosm of the US
industry, can perhaps provide us with an answer. This
company has products as diverse as car parts, semiconduct-
ors and financial and information services. Some 150 products of this US$6 billion conglomerate were compared with
nearly 600 competing products in terms of the customers'
perception of quality, recording at the same time the return
to the company on the assets employed. So now we are
trying to relate quality to profit: and profit is in effect the
ultimate measure of productivity. A high profit must mean
high productivity, and *vice versa*. TRW excelled when this
comparison was made. The best of the TRW products (best
in terms of the customer rating) earned three times the

return on the assets employed, when compared to the competitive products. The return on sales showed a similar pattern. These figures demonstrate that it *is* possible to maintain productivity whilst maintaining quality and high earnings.

What is more, the customer is *looking* for quality. An independent survey by the American Society for Quality Control confirmed that customers are willing to pay more, far more, for quality than is normally anticipated by the manufacturers or even the quality experts. The premium that would be paid actually varied greatly with the product. The results of this survey are shown in Table 19.1. The premium that customers were willing to pay is expressed as a percentage over the original price.

	Premium %	Customers not willing to pay extra premium %
Quality cars:	33	10
Better quality dishwasher:	50	4
Better TV set:	65	6
Better quality sofa:	75	4
High quality shoes:	140	3

Table 19.1

These figures are most interesting. It seems that, generally speaking, ever fewer people were unwilling to pay a premium, as the size of the premium people were prepared to pay increased.

The survey also disclosed that people in the higher income brackets were by far the most dissatisfied with the quality of American products. You can see why. They were prepared and able to pay for high quality, but couldn't find it on the market. If we add to the fact that high quality will bring a higher price and hence a higher profit, the further fact that 'quality is free', as we have just demonstrated in Chapter 18, then one wonders why more American firms are not pressing forward to improve the quality of their products. Some firms are, of course: we have just demonstrated that the TRW conglomerate have done just that. It all sounds so simple. Better quality, higher productivity, higher profits: all the result of worker satisfaction and good team morale. And it costs nothing: in fact, it pays dividends. Everyone can come out a winner – management, workers and customers – yet so many companies fail to follow the team approach and apply the principles we have been discussing for the sake of better quality and higher productivity.

IBM'S QUALITY PROGRAMME

Let us see how it works out once again in action, taking IBM as our example. We have already pointed out that IBM are outstanding in their field, and we have also seen that the secret of their success is not technology as such, but people. This is, of course, our underlying theme throughout this book: that it is people, rather than the technology or techniques, that count. The human factor is all-important. When it comes to IBM, we are indebted to a report by H J Harrington (1986) for details of the way in which IBM achieved excellence. Let us cite a few examples.

Error-free installations

Through proper focusing on this issue, putting a project team on the problem in relation to new products, IBM have achieved what was hitherto thought to be impossible – an error-free installation.

Innovation has no limit

There is no limit to what can be achieved, even with mature products, such as flat ribbon cables. These are the product of a well-established technology, but there was always massive reworking. Inspired by one industrial engineer, a team was set up specifically to attack this area. The result: reworking fell from 25 per cent to a mere 4 per cent and problems on final testing from 12 per cent to 1.2 per cent, a breakthrough indeed and the payback on this effort must have come in only a few months.

The quest for improvement

Improvement need not be confined to the technical products. The most impressive results were obtained even with accountancy procedures. Whilst they were said to have 98 per cent success rate in data entry, nevertheless they had some 30,000 miscodes a day. Persistent efforts over a two-year period actually reduced this figure to a fifth of what it was before. Or, to put it another way, their accuracy rose to 99.6 per cent: a substantial increase over the earlier figure.

Software coding

The number of defects per 1000 lines of code was reduced, over a six-year period, by two-thirds.

Speaking the suppliers' language

IBM found that they erred when talking to their suppliers, by using such terms as 'Acceptable Quality Levels' (AQLs). What the supplier was interested in was the permissible errors, expressed in parts per million. Once they started using the supplier's language, there was a major drop in defects: 93 per cent on transistors, 98 per cent on transformers and 99 per cent on capacitors, all tending towards the ideal of zero defects.

IBM also revolutionised their approach when dealing with the customer, and in this a number of the more successful companies were with them. The practice used to be to draw up a specification and submit it to the customer. But it was eventually realised that this was a most roundabout and time-wasting approach, since of course the customer came back with a multitude of queries and suggestions. Now they ask the customer to provide beforehand a specification of his requirements, and see what they can do to meet it. The customer knows what he wants, especially in terms of quality, and no amount of independent product testing will provide an answer to that question. Once the customer has said what he wants, the company can do its best to meet the requirements. This emphasises once again a basic principle: always listen to the customer!

WHAT HAPPENS WITH RESEARCH AND DEVELOPMENT?

Research and development (R&D) is very difficult to assess in terms of quality and productivity. Nevertheless it can be done, and should be done. Allen *et al* (1988) have reported on the extensive research work on R&D carried out at the A P Sloan School of the Massachusetts Institute of Technology (MIT). Their work has highlighted the importance of maintaining a close link between the project team and the main objectives when dealing with an R&D project. A sample of 181 teams was studied, including in all some 2000 team members, coming from a wide variety of R&D organisations. The objective of the research was to select the most effective teams and then determine the secret of their success. The assessment of success in R&D is difficult, but the approach used was broadly as follows:

- each team's performance was assessed by a senior member in its own organisation;

- the experience of the team was assessed by noting the average time spent by each individual on research;

- a questionnaire was completed by all the participants.

There were some surprising conclusions. For instance, it was found that there was no clear evidence of a direct relationship between performance and experience, or period of tenure, though some teams with extended experience did perform much better than others, and certainly better than newly-formed teams. On further investigation this was found to be actually more related to the extent to which the functional manager, or project manager, looked after his team. In particular, the extent to which he ensured that they were kept fully abreast of research work in their respective areas of expertise. But it was also said that the primary role of the project manager was to ensure that the team members had their attention constantly focused on the aims and objectives of the research project they had in hand.

The importance of the project manager or functional manager in relation to the effectiveness of research teams has always been recognised. Team members are normally put on a project from another department, and then work directly for the project manager. But at the same time they retain a powerful link with the head of their department, to which they will return in due course. This present research into the operation of research teams sought to confirm and emphasise the role the project manager plays in the success of the team, and it was seen that he did indeed exert a most powerful influence. The project manager's role was thus vital. He had to ensure that:

– the team and the organisation were in synchronisation;

– the organisation must have complete commitment to the research team's efforts;

– there must be no rotation of project managers;

– the team must be able to interface with other members of the organisation effectively.

What we learn is that whilst there is no sensible way to assess quality and productivity when we come to research teams – their profitability can never be assessed – yet their efficiency can still be measured. From this we learn, once again, that the project manager, or leader, plays a most significant role. There was certainly a marked difference between newly-formed teams, and teams that had been in the business for a good while, thus demonstrating that experience also has a most significant part to play. But there remain significant differences between research teams and the rest of teams in industry. Quality and productivity in

Research and Development cannot be easily and properly assessed, nor can they be rewarded.

USE OF INCENTIVES

Yet it is a sound principle that productivity and quality should be properly rewarded. Motivation is a very positive force, and reward undoubtedly increases motivation. Human nature is very complex, and it is difficult to determine exactly what it is that motivates individuals. It is clear, as we demonstrate in Chapter 21, that work involvement ensures higher quality, better productivity and innovation, but how does one ensure that there is involvement?

Financial incentives are a considerable help. Unfortunately, financial incentives can often become counter-productive, since incentives for individuals are not the same as incentives for teams. After all, a good team realises that its success is due to team effort, not the isolated efforts of specific individuals in the team.

Whilst it has been established that above-average pay does yield above-average results, there is no certainty that this operates on a pro-rata basis. No one really knows, but it seems likely, as in almost any field, that there must be a point of diminishing returns. Additional incentives will certainly encourage people to take on a number of different jobs, and the more ambitious will stand out above the others, but this is not necessarily a good thing. Of more importance is the team, and its concerted effort: incentives should never be so designed as to destroy the team concept, since that is crucial to success.

A company profit-sharing scheme can be a very effective way of providing incentive, and about a quarter of the base pay seems an appropriate amount to provide proper incentive. The relationship between the incentive and the actual performance, though not simple, must be clearly recognised. It is important that incentive payments, such as profit sharing, are prompt. Delay means that they can no longer be related by the individual to the effort that he has put in, or the output of the company that actually resulted in the profits being shared. An employee share-ownership plan is another method of providing incentive. This seems to yield very positive results, with the participants feeling that they have a direct stake in the company and its prosperity.

A poll of American and Japanese workers in this context has been quite revealing. In response to the statement: 'I have an inner need to do the best I can, regardless of pay', the American workers did substantially better than their Japanese counterparts. This was a rather unexpected result. However, the situation was reversed when the question was put: 'Who would benefit the most from an increase in worker productivity?' Only 9 per cent of the American workers thought they would benefit, whereas some 93 per cent of the Japanese workers thought they would.

This demonstrates that the incentives offered in America, as assessed by the workers, were far fewer than those offered in Japan. Or perhaps it had more to do with a sense of participation. In Japan, it seems, the workers may well put their company's interests above their own personal interests, especially since they know that these latter are well looked after by the company. The answer to the second question may also indicate that American workers do not really trust their management to share any increase in profits equitably and this, of course, is a matter of great concern.

It seems that there are two major factors that may increase the commitment of Japanese workers:

- there is a traditional 25 to 50 per cent bonus at the end of a good year. This certainly creates a feeling that hard work is being adequately rewarded.
- the total sum distributed by the company as a bonus usually exceeds the company's after-bonus profit.

There is nothing new about such an approach to incentives. The concept has been long known in the United States. Peters (1987) mentions that in 1887 Proctor and Gamble, introducing a profit-sharing plan to its employees, said:

The chief problem of big business today is to shape

its policies so that each worker will feel that he is a vital part of his company with a personal responsibility for its success *and a chance to share in that process.*

Unfortunately this principle is often ignored. Very few companies in the United States apply it seriously, and give their employees a real, substantial share in the profits of the company. Current assessments are that only some 20 per cent of the total workforce in the United States participates in profit distribution or some similar scheme. In Japan, by contrast, participation in the profits is indeed an incentive that is very widely employed, one of many factors that have contributed to the success of Japanese industry.

WHY THE JAPANESE EXCEL

We cannot leave the subject of productivity without taking a further look at Japanese industry, seeking to see why they have been so successful, out-producing the rest of the world. They manage to maintain quality whilst continually increasing productivity. Within some 40 years Japan has grown from practically nothing to lead the world, with ever-increasing economic power. The Japanese success has created a yardstick by which the performance, quality, productivity and teamwork of all the other nations is being measured. It seems that today every nation wants to emulate Japan, hoping that they can achieve the degree of economic success and prosperity that she has achieved. But how has it been done?

The best way to assess the achievements of Japan is to compare it with another country, and we have chosen to compare what has been done in Japan with what is done in the United States. This has been the subject of a comprehensive research paper from the Rutgers University, Newark, NJ, sponsored by the United States National Science Foundation and the Japan Youth Research Institute. The findings of this research paper have been publicised by Hull *et al* (1988).

This research work compares 1982 data on New Jersey

factories (some 80) that survived from a 1973 sample of 110 factories with 94 Japanese factories operating in the 1980s, none of these having closed down in the preceding ten years. It seems that when factories close down in the United States, the bulk of the workers become jobless, whereas in Japan not only are closures far more rare, but no one loses their job when it does happen. Some of the Japanese companies did change their products – for instance from ballpoint pens to robotics – but they retrained their workforce to cope with the new jobs. No one was dismissed.

Overall the major points of difference that seemed to account for the Japanese factories consistently outperforming their American counterparts can be summarised as follows:

- sound human resource development;

- provision of motivating incentives;

- a willingness to work;

- proper marketing of output and buying of raw materials;

- efficient methods of production, including automation wherever possible.

There is no doubt that many other nations, apart from the United States, have sought to emulate Japanese techniques, such as we have just outlined above, in order that they may become competitive in world markets. Although some companies have been successful in this, at times undercutting Japanese costs, they seem to have great difficulty in matching Japanese quality. The results of the research outlined above demonstrate that the basic failure lies in generating the appropriate motivation. This may seem a minor factor, but it is of major importance. It will also be noticed that the first three factors set out above are all people related.

The Japanese companies use in-house training programmes, retraining at regular intervals, and all this extends to the assembly line worker. Indeed it embraces *all* the workers in a company. In sharp contrast, very few American and European companies use in-house training to any extent: IBM is a notable exception to this rule. What is more, such training as does exist seldom reaches the shop floor.

Some other points that came out of the research that deserve emphasis are:

Emphasis on group rewards

There is greater emphasis in Japan on group rewards, provided in addition to personal incentives. Managers and workers are placed in the same position when it comes to reward, and this encourages a sense of togetherness. This causes the worker to feel that he belongs, and there is a feeling of solidarity with his company. The US companies, on the other hand, had poor incentive schemes, and they failed to link productivity gains by their employees with an improvement in rewards.

Company unity

The solidarity between managers and workers in Japan is further promoted by the relatively small wage differentials. What is more, shop floor personnel are all on monthly salaries: this further blurs the distinction between staff and worker. Other unifying techniques used in Japanese companies include the morning ceremony of calisthenics, and the joint singing of the company song at the workplace. As a result, employees tend to relate closely both to all their fellow employees and to their company.

The suggestion box

There are a great many more suggestions made by employees in Japan than in the United States. The figure is said to be over 11 suggestions per worker in Japan, as compared with 0.2 per worker in the United States. In saying this, it should not be forgotten that the ratio of workers to management is much higher in Japan. There the workers comprise more than 80 per cent of the total staff, so the difference in the number of suggestions made is even greater than at first appears. The motivation for making suggestions seems to lie in the fact that the Japanese worker has a real sense of belonging to his comany. He is proud of contributing to its success by improving quality or productivity: the main theme of most of the suggestions that are made.

It is interesting to note that the two sets of factories that were the subject of research were roughly comparable in terms of product types and size. There were major differences in relation to the use of quality circles and innovation, which we shall discuss in later chapters. Meanwhile, let us introduce a note of caution. Imitation of the Japanese management techniques is *not* a solution to management problems in the United States or elsewhere in the world. Whilst the rest of the world may have much to learn from Japan, one has to be careful to decide what. It is the principles, rather than the actual practice involved in their management style, that can be usefully copied.

20 Applying the Principles

SUMMARY

This part of the book, comprising four chapters, deals with team participation. Chapter 18 dealt with the significance of quality and Chapter 19 with the related subject of productivity. Now we come to consider the application of these principles, primarily by the use of what have become known as quality circles. It is the quality circle that gives a company quality control. We are looking at multi-disciplinary teams concerned solely with quality: seeing how they work and how certain companies and countries, such as Japan, have made the most effective use of quality circles.

THE QUALITY CIRCLE

Sound quality control is really an exercise in team building, the prime cause of the Japanese economic miracle. It was established that sound quality control, instead of costing a company money, actually saved money. Whilst the increased intensity of quality control calls for increased effort and hence increased cost, the saving in relation to dealing with rejects and reworking offset this. What is more, the company enhances its reputation, improves sales, so that turnover and profits increase.

This improvement in quality control is achieved by the *quality circle*, as it has become known. The quality circle is, in effect, a very special type of team, developed for the specific purpose of maintaining quality in factory production. It is a very good illustration of the team-building exercise, because the team has very clear objectives. A quality circle can very quickly justify its existence on financial grounds: it is contributing to the profits of the company. Quality, like safety, is essentially an attitude of mind. Just as safety can pay, so does the maintenance of quality pay. In the case of quality maintenance, the fact that it does indeed contribute to the profits of the company has been demonstrated time and again. (Unfortunately in the case of safety the demonstration is by no means as easy, although perhaps major disasters, such as Bhopal and Chernobyl, are beginning to drive home that particular point.)

Unlike the normal project team, which is usually involved in a wide range of subjects, the quality circle is involved with one subject only. A quality circle usually consists of some eight to ten members having the appropriate skills, and is concerned with making specific recommendations for the improvement of an existing operation or product. The real payoff in relation to the work of the quality circle comes in the reduction in the rejection rate and the minimisation of reworking. The objective is to make the item as perfect as possible in the first place.

Whilst the quality circle was originally applied to production, it has since been extended to other departments, including service departments and service companies. Indeed it can be extended to *all* departments and companies, as indeed has happened in Japan. This has the result that every member of the company is then a member of one or other of the quality circles that have been set up. The quality circle can also be seen as part of an overall approach to problem solving, and it is very possible that the concept may eventually completely replace the traditional pyramidal company structure. To quote Naisbitt (1982):

> The failures of hierarchies to solve society's problems forced people to talk to one another – and this was the beginning of networks.

Quality circles are very helpful in problem solving, since they are very closely related to the nature of the job and those doing it. Quality circles, in the course of their regular meetings, help to identify problems and then seek the appropriate solutions through the application of their functional expertise. What is more, they are in a position to implement their suggestions, in the cause of better quality. But at the same time a stubborn problem can have been solved.

The introduction of a quality circle, a radical departure from convention, is not easy, and this can cost a lot of time and money. It is a 'bottom up' approach, rather than the much more conventional 'top down' approach.

There is no doubt, however, that shopfloor problems are best solved at the level where they occur, where their nature is fully understood and appreciated. This is despite the fact that senior management is normally considered to be the proper centre for all new ideas. However, the quality circle principle has its limitations. It cannot be effectively implemented within a system which has a very strong hierarchical system, such as the armed forces, the police, or the civil services. Effective worker participation, which is the key to an effective quality circle, requires the right climate and the appropriate leadership style. These are just not there in strongly hierarchical systems.

What is more, managers and supervisors must be fully committed to the quality circle concept for it to be a success, and even then miracles will not happen overnight. Failures have been known to occur, and one has to be very careful when first introducing the concept of the quality circle.

Whilst the term quality circle is almost universally recognised, other names have been used for the concept. For instance, at Honeywell they are called PTPs (Production Team Programmes). Other names, apart from the simple term 'teams', include Productivity Improvement Teams, Involvement Teams and Participative Quality Teams. The name will depend to some extent on the specific purpose for which the teams are set up. But whilst we are praising the objectives and the successful way in which the quality circle is being used, let us not forget that it is not the universal answer. There is no such thing as the 'quick fix' in this context.

The quality circle is a specific management philosophy which can contribute creatively to the solution of operational problems. We have mentioned the American conglomerate TRW before as an outstanding example of productivity, following upon the development of teams. It is said that following the introduction of quality circles at that company, the absentee rate fell from six to two per cent, whilst production increased by some 35 per cent. The point we make here is that the impact of the quality circle extends well beyond the simple establishment of sound quality control and the consequent improvement in quality. There are quite a range of incidental benefits, brought about by the growing team spirit, which is an essential part of the quality circle.

MAINTAINING AND IMPROVING QUALITY

Despite the incidental benefits, the primary role of the quality circle must be to maintain and improve quality, taking that word in the broadest possible sense. This can be seen as creative problem solving. Quality failure presents problems, which can be solved by taking steps for quality improvement. The team has to use all the available facts, even if they are inadequate and then seek more facts if that is felt to be necessary. The team is in fact involved in a sort of 'brainstorming' operation, so brainstorming techniques can help.

Disagreement can lead either to hard feelings or to innovation, depending largely on the sense of purpose which imbues the team. The clash of ideas should be encouraged, but the clash of personalities discouraged. Idea evaluation should be kept completely separate from idea generation, since criticism of the initial idea inhibits creative thinking. Teams, like committees, are not in themselves creative. Creativity is very much an individual matter, but groups and teams can not only provide a forum for creative thinking, but stimulate it. Each member of the team will have a profile of strengths and weaknesses, but there is no such thing as the 'complete thinker'. Some are better than others at one or other of the various types of thinking that eventually lead to creative thought.

The relevant mental skills are: analysing, reasoning, synthesising, holistic thinking, valuing, intuitive memory, creativity, and numeracy. The utmost care must be taken not to stifle a good idea. The story of the postage stamp is very relevant to this context. Roland Hill, the inventor of the postage stamp, was reported as saying:

> [what is wanted is] a piece of paper just large enough to bear the stamp, covered at the back with a glutinous wash, which the sender might, by applying a little moisture, attach to the back of the letter.

What was the reaction of the Postmaster General of the day? 'Of all the wild and visionary schemes I have ever heard of, or read of, this is the most extravagant.'

The maintenance and improvement of quality is fundamentally a management problem. We have just seen, with the postage stamp, how management failed to recognise a good idea when it saw one, and this is always happening. Pall (1987), writing on quality management, claims to deal adequately with the 'successful management of quality'. People are seen to be the key to this, and the successful management of quality must therefore focus on the successful motivation and commitment of people.

Quality is essential to ensure both the competitiveness and the profitability of a company, and will pay handsome dividends in this respect. But the concept of quality management must recognise its dependence on people, and that quality assurance can be expected to bring increased competitiveness and profitability. All too often all the attention is given to quality improvement, overlooking the related benefits that will also come if it is managed properly. Hansen and Ghare (1987) bring us another view of the techniques of quality control, a sequel to an earlier book (Hansen, 1963). Many of the case studies in the earlier book are repeated in the second book, the author's excuse being that 'like good management, good quality control is never out of date'.

But what exactly is quality control? If we are considering

the maintenance and improvement of quality, this certainly calls for control. Good quality control involves various management techniques and devices which are used to monitor and hence control the various steps involved in the planning, design, production and checking of a product before it is offered for sale. Japan and West Germany have come to represent the ideal in terms of high quality, which it seems has at the same time led to lower costs. Even though quality must be considered as 'everybody's job', yet it seems that total quality control revolves around the supervisor on the shop floor. Top management's total commitment to quality is a must, but that alone is not enough. Cooperation on the shop floor is also essential, and it is the local supervisor who brings that about. The supervisor becomes the leader of the team there, who are primarily responsible for the product and its quality.

QUALITY IS CRUCIAL

Quality control involves what we might call a 'thought revolution', which helps to prevent mismanagement. It has also led to some unusual but very effective management systems, such as that called the 'just in time' (JIT). JIT helps, for instance, to reduce inventory levels of raw materials to the minimum, by arranging phased delivery that closely matches the actual requirements. In other words, the raw materials are ordered 'just in time'.

It is suggested that quality control has proved effective in every field where it has been applied. It is not only applicable to the workplace, but is a social phenomenon that can be applied to politics and to one's personal life. Why is this? Because the crux of quality control policy is 'prevention is better than cure', and that is clearly a principle of universal application. But do not be misled: quality control is not a tool – it is an objective and a mission. To attain this objective a wide variety of tools will be needed, such as industrial engineering and operational research. It will then become a practical discipline that is, fortunately, consistent with human nature. That is why it is so readily accepted once it is properly applied.

It is also clear that companies that ignore this issue of quality and quality control are commiting what is tantamount to 'corporate suicide'. This is the primary point made by Shetty and Buehler (1987), writing on quality, productivity and innovation. They describe strategies for gaining a competitive advantage and present us with a formidable list of successful companies who have set the pace in this area. The three vital factors, quality, productivity and innovation, are seen to be closely interrelated. They are absolutely essential if progress is to be sustained, and they can only be achieved through the complete commitment of the top management and the complete conviction of all the employees, with close cooperation and team effort in all departments.

THE GUIDE TO QUALITY

We have had a lot to say about the benefits of quality, quality control and quality circles, but how does one set about improving upon the existing situation? How does one ensure that quality control pervades the company? Well, it so happens that we are not short of guidance. A number of books have been written specifically for this purpose: to guide the uninitiated along the right paths. Typical of these is *Quality Circles Master Guide* by Sud Ingle (1985). The basis of this guide is the way in which quality control is handled in Japan. Whilst the concept has made great strides in Japan, the author asserts that the approach is valid for all cultures, summed up in the words: 'If Japan can, why can't we?' We cannot enlarge on the guidance given: you must read the book. But it is said that the concept is moving rapidly across the world. Countries such as Belgium, Brazil, Denmark, Malaysia, Mexico, The Netherlands, Taiwan, Thailand, the UK and the USA have all begun to apply the concept.

Another book on the same theme, by Robson (1982), is titled *Quality Circles – A Practical Guide*. This is an excellent introduction to both the philosophy and practice of quality circles. The author seeks to answer the sceptics who ask 'Will it work for me?' by presenting a series of case histories across a wide range of industries, demonstrating the way in which the quality circle concept has helped all these companies with their problems. The range is wide. The companies cited are not confined to manufacturing industry. Banks, insurance companies and retailing organisations have all benefited from the application of the principles of quality control by introducing the quality circle.

Let us conclude this section on the guides that are available by mentioning just one more from the many, Hutchins' *Quality Circles Handbook* (1985). This author has been intimately involved in the introduction and propagation of this particular technique in British industry. The book describes the author's experiences, together with those of his colleagues and friends. Within the first year of taking up this 'quality mission' fifteen companies had been trained in the technique, and the number had grown to more than 100 in the UK alone by 1984. We mentioned, in Chapter 18, the famous Kaoru Ishikawa and his influence on the development of quality in production. Back in 1979 a three-day conference on quality circles was organised in London by Hutchins, at which Kaoru Ishikawa spoke. He said: 'Don't expect too much. If you are able to encourage just two companies to take up the concept within a year, you will be doing very well'. Hutchins did far better than that. His book carries a Preface by Dr J M Juran, author of the prestigious *Quality Control Handbook* (1974), where he says:

> The Quality Control Circle movement is a tremendous one, which no other country seems able to imitate. Through the development of this movement Japan will be swept into world leadership in quality.

Of course this has already happened, and the rest is history. But other countries are now learning the technique fast, as we have just seen. Whether they will learn the lessons fast enough to catch up with Japan remains to be seen. They certainly have a long way to go!

It should of course be made clear that quality control is intended to strengthen existing systems, not to replace them. It represents no threat to anyone, not even to the trade unions. The basic intent is to create a healthy and more cooperative work environment. Experience has indeed shown that the setting up of quality circles does not interfere with any legitimate union interest. To encourage continuing good work, those responsible for quality control should be respected and appreciated, and their contribution recognised, but financial reward *must* be avoided. That is not what it is all about. Indeed, increased financial reward could even detract from the effectivenes of such schemes. Quality control as advocated here does not replace the company-wide quality control activity: it is designed to supplement and reinforce it. Great care is needed in introducing quality control: it must not be done in a hurry. Considerable preplanning and in-company discussion is an essential prerequisite to its success.

QUALITY CIRCLES NOT A UNIVERSAL PANACEA

It has to be recognised that intensive quality control and the establishment of quality circles is not always the answer. There has been extensive research comparing American industry with Japanese industry, and it is apparent that the differences between the use of quality circles in these two countries can only be partly responsible for the differences in productivity and profitability. The differences are far too many for a simple answer to this particular dilemma. One has to go beyond the mere establishment of quality circles, and consider in depth the basic work structure and the way it motivates employees.

Whilst the quality circle concept has been applied with a considerable measure of success in the construction industry, first in Japan and more recently in the United States, success cannot be assured. Gully *et al* (1987) point out in an excellent article on the application of quality control circles to construction that with the inevitable uniqueness of each construction site and the wide variability in the workforce from site to site, it is difficult to apply the classic quality circle concept. However, if the concept is modified to meet the changing circumstances, as outlined in the article, then the chances of success are greatly improved. So we finish with a warning: quality control circles cannot be universally applied.

21 Involvement and Commitment

SUMMARY

We now come to the close of the sequence of chapters dealing with team participation and also come to the end of the book. We have looked at quality, then the allied subject of productivity, and then the use of total quality control and quality circles. Now we take the discussion further by reviewing yet another related aspect, namely the involvement of the individual members of the team, and its relation to innovation. Innovation, it seems, is basically dependent upon people's involvement and commitment. We have therefore to set it in that context so that we can understand how to make innovation flourish. We see that the key to success is for a company to have a cause and then communicate that cause to all its employees, thus ensuring their commitment.

THE CONNECTING LINK

Productivity is an abstract term and can mean many different things to different people. One's view of productivity depends very much upon one's viewpoint. Even its definition depends upon the definer. The economist, the engineer and the accountant all have very different views of productivity. Broadly speaking, however, productivity can be defined as output per unit of input, say worker manhour. The higher this ratio is, the greater the productivity, all other things being equal. When thus defined, productivity is known to be higher in Japan than in the United States, and this has been ascribed to three major factors:

- a greater extent of automation;
- greater effort by the workers;
- the workers' involvement and commitment.

Quality, as we have seen in the previous three chapters, usually implies complete conformity with the specification, or zero defects. This means that quality is in essence an attribute of productivity: without high quality productivity must fall. We have also seen that quality is determined not only by the sophistication of the manufacturing equipment, but also by the attitude of the workers. Indeed, we have asserted that the worker's attitude is the most important factor of all. The work offered to the worker should be so designed that he is responsible for the quality of his work, and hence the product. It is, however, extremely difficult to assess and measure quality in any absolute sense. Indeed, it has to be measured negatively, by assessing the absence of defects. Zero defects means perfect quality.

Thus far productivity and quality: they are closely inter-related. The third factor in the equation, innovation, refers typically to the invention of new products and processes, and their successful commercialisation. Some studies have indicated that Japan lags behind the United States when it comes to innovation and inventiveness. This may, however, be an erroneous conclusion, although it is quite popular. Azumi (1986), for instance, found that the normal Western assessments of innovation tended to discount the great number of small product and process improvements initi-ated by Japanese employees. Collectively, of course, they can be substantial and we cannot ignore what we might call the 'proof of the pudding'. There is no doubt that Japan is ahead of the West in many a product line and this differen-tial is growing. And much of their advance can be attributed to innovation.

Now let us consider these three factors, productivity, quality and innovation, and examine their interrelation-ship. There is usually a trade-off between productivity improvement and innovation, at least in the short term.

Quality, too, is a performance variable, affected by both innovation and productivity.

YOU GET WHAT YOU EXPECT

When we come to consider people's involvement and commitment to their work, there is a very simple adage which should never be forgotten. This asserts that a person performs as you expect the person to perform. Or, to put it the way it really happens, a person does what you expect of him: rarely more than you expect of him. This is a very simple truth, but it is often forgotton. Some studies of managerial relationships have shown that merely the expressed interest of a manager in what is happening in his department can lead to an increase in productivity. But this simplistic conclusion has long since been disproved. Long-term and sustained improvement is only possible if the manager's attention is accompanied by a genuine belief (or perhaps, a displayed belief) in the abilities of his team. To put it simply, positive expectations bring positive results. The converse is also true, most unfortunately. Negative expectations bring negative results.

This is the so-called Pygmalion effect, so named after a certain king of Cyprus. Mythology tells us that the king sculpted a statue of a woman that embodied all his own desires and expectations. His repeated overtures to the gods finally resulted in life being breathed into his statue. George Bernard Shaw also took up this theme in his play Pygmalion, where a professor transforms a cockney flower girl into an aristocratic woman. It has further been asserted on the basis of research that student performance is far more in accord with the teacher's expectations than with their own natural ability. The significance of all this is that it demonstrates the belief, which we accept, that expectation plays a most significant role when you are dealing with people. Expectation, therefore, must have a powerful influence on all the three aspects we are dealing with here, namely quality, productivity and innovation.

This concept of the role of 'expectation' has been used

with great advantage in corporate situations, and is an essential element in all teamwork. Many companies now recognise that in people lies their greatest resource. It behoves them, therefore, to pay a great deal of attention to their people, seeking to get the best from them. This will be achieved if they *expect* the best. One expects the best if one has a good opinion of one's employees, and they will then meet expectations. It is much like a self-fulfilling prophecy, a concept which has been confirmed by numerous research projects. One case that is cited is where school children were arbitrarily divided into two groups, one labelled as intelligent and the other as below average. In every case the first group performed much better than the second. This has been explained as follows:

> Teachers encourage greater responsiveness from students of whom they expect more. They call on such students more often, ask them harder questions, give them more time to answer, and prompt them to the correct answer.

In other words, expecting more of them, they demand more, and get it. What is true of children and their teachers is also true of managers and their employees. Those managers who expect and look for the best from their employees will get it, too.

Looking at the problem for a moment from the point of view of the one who is required to have such expectations and make them plain, they should be sincere, since one's expectations determine how one will behave in a given situation. If the leader, for instance, enters a meeting with positive expectations, the team members are immediately and more or less automatically encouraged to participate to the full. There are other ways to encourage such participation:

-   ask open-ended questions;
-   use silence when appropriate, such as waiting for an answer;
-   redirect questions asked of the leader to other team members;

- avoid win/lose situations;
- make eye contact;
- use humour when appropriate;
- be very willing to listen to the viewpoint of others.

On the other hand, there are a number of what we would call 'killer' phrases which should never be used, such as that it is 'contrary to policy', or 'it just won't work', or the most devastating of all: 'we have never done it before'. The simple answer to that, of course, is that now is the time to try.

PERFORMANCE FOLLOWS COMMITMENT

We are concerned with performance, high performance, in all the areas we have been considering: productivity, quality and innovation. How does one increase performance? It seems that performance is wholly dependent upon employee attitudes, and the key employee attitude is that of commitment. For commitment one needs a cause, and this cause must be subscribed to by all the employees of the company. What is more, they must accept and agree that it is a desirable cause. The cause does not have to continually stay the same. It should be reviewed periodically and the results of the review should be conveyed, once again, to all the employees. They will then maintain their commitment to the company and the 'causes' its espouses. Management cannot 'order' commitment, but it can get people involved by translating the overall company cause into specific actions relating to small groups, and then see it spread. These actions then become their immediate objective, and an attainable objective, but they see their personal objective as contributing directly to the company 'cause'. Once commitment has been brought about, management should be able to change course as and when required, replacing one objective with another, without the commitment of their employees being diminshed in any way.

We have just said that a company 'cause' must be reduced, or transformed, into specific objectives meaningful to the people who are actually carrying out the work, and this is most important. For involvement, commitment and the consequent cooperation, managers must so design the work that it is meaningful to the people involved. The more usual slogans, such as 'more profit' or 'continued growth', are meaningless to the average employee. They carry no more weight than the obsolete and vague phrase 'we are serving the shareholder'. This may well be true, but it does not relate to the day-to-day work being carried out by the employee. The objectives set before the worker must be meaningful to him, and relate to the workplace, if companies are to 'renew' themselves. John Egan, on taking charge of Jaguar, the British car company, was faced with a host of serious problems, including a company-wide strike and heavy losses. Since he could not tackle too many problems at one time, he decided to focus his attention on just one single key issue: quality. It worked!

Jaguar manufactures luxury cars, but its image had suffered badly during the late 1970s and early 1980s. The standing joke, it appeared, was that you needed two Jaguars: one to drive whilst the other was under repair. To assess the problem in their push for quality, Jaguar obtained extensive feedback from a sample of one hundred Jaguar customers, sampling at the same time a hundred Mercedes Benz owners and a hundred BMW owners, the companies which were their major competitors in the quality car market. In the case of Jaguar the survey provided a long list of some 200 defects, including poor paintwork, steering gear that leaked, gear boxes that failed, and so on. John Egan focused the attention of the whole company both on these defects of quality and on the quality attributes of their competitors, set up quality circles, and got it all put right. Then the company went on from success to success.

The case of Jaguar demonstrates that to achieve success it is necessary for a company to have a cause: in their case, quality. As we have said before, it needs to be a cause that *everyone* can understand, appreciate and relate to in their everyday work: quality is such a cause. This approach has been the secret of success not only with Jaguar, but with many other well-known companies, such as Olivetti, Hewlett Packard and Ford. We can even include a symphony orchestra in the list: the San Francisco Symphony Orchestra. This concept is by no means restricted to manufacturing companies. But it has to be realised that there can be no let-up: the pursuit of quality has to be persistent and continuous. All this is aptly summed up by a notice said to be displayed in H Ross Perot's (of General Motors fame) office:

> Every good and excellent thing stands moment by moment on the razor's edge of danger and must be fought for.

Renewal is a constant challenge: you can never sit back and relax.

FROM BOMBS TO FISHING RODS

We have said that for the proper development of the quality-productivity-innovation triangle, there must be commitment. And for commitment you must have a cause. This is well illustrated by a very interesting case: ZEBCO (originally the Zero Hour Bomb Company). This company used to make bombs for the fracturing of oil wells and it was failing. In their quest for diversification, they took on the manufacture of fishing rods. How did this happen? It is said that an inventor of a new innovative type of fishing rod walked into ZEBCO's office with a sample, a toolroom specialist tried out the reel in the company's parking lot and found it worked well. So the company decided to take up the manufacture of the fishing rod. This led to a remarkable turnaround and company renewal. There was a strong commitment by all the employees, with great improvements in both quality and productivity, and it all came about through innovation: the introduction of a radically different product.

ZEBCO was started up in 1949, and had remarkable growth for some 25 years, but the 1974 oil crisis caused the 'bomb' business to collapse. But at the same time fishing reels were not doing too well. Foreign competition had intensified, with fishing reels being 'dumped' on the market. This resulted in a vast surplus during the early 1980s, and fishing reels were selling at US$10 a piece. It was a

question of 'survival of the fittest' and the workers at
ZEBCO took up the challenge. The situation was indeed one
they could easily comprehend. The route to survival lay in
reducing costs and improving both quality and productivity. But this concept had to be conveyed to all the employees.

It was felt that the impact of the message would be lost if
it was communicated via a circular, posting a notice, or
calling all the employees together for a large meeting. So Jim
Dawson, vice-president of manufacturing, called the employees together in groups of four at a time, taking them into
his confidence in respect of the new product line, thus
getting them committed to the cause – working for the
survival of the company. This consultation process was a
very time-consuming job – it took nearly two years in all –
but it succeeded. The ZEBCO management is reported as
saying:

> We took the time to visit with the people and let
> them know what we were doing and why. We
> taught them that quality starts within and that
> they should try to work smarter, not harder... We
> asked everyone what they needed to do their job
> better. They told us: 'Give us better parts and tools,
> and have them here when we need them'. We
> discovered that 85 per cent of our problems were
> rooted in bad parts from suppliers:

So here was a situation which, properly handled by management, not only led to commitment by the staff, but
highlighted the real problem. It was a problem that was
readily solved, with the result that costs were slashed and
productivity (measured in the number of reels produced
per person per day) was tripled. ZEBCO attributed their
success to three vital factors:

- Management's conviction that everyone wants to
  contribute and will contribute if in the process his
  contribution is recognised.

- The cause was linked to a commitment: a commitment with which the workers could identify. The
  face-to-face meetings in small groups resulted in

management and workers listening to one another for the first time. Later they could see the real results of their joint action.

- Positive action followed once the real bottleneck was identified. Suppliers were approached and the position was explained to them – they were made part of the team. Eventually, they too benefited, producing better quality items at a lower cost.

THE NEED FOR INVOLVEMENT

It seems that we cannot over-stress the importance and significance of involvement. The case of ZEBCO illustrates the power of involvement very clearly. Everyone concerned should be involved, not only the employees but the suppliers and even the customers. Involvement, it seems, brings innovation. No matter how mature a company or its products, there are a multitude of opportunities for innovation. These are not necessarily in the realm of research and development, but come from the daily, routine, humdrum operations. Involvement should lead to innovative ideas, designed to increase productivity or improve quality, and these should be encouraged. Innovation must become a way of life at the workplace, but for it to be a success people must be given ample time to think, and plenty of freedom.

It is interesting to see that managements in Japan, and more lately in the United States and West Germany, are insisting that their engineers spend a great deal of their time on the shop floor, instead of in their airconditioned cabins. Only then do they get a feel for what is actually happening on the shop floor and the problems faced by the workers. This can lead immediately to improvements, both minor and major, and that is the way innovation is brought about. It comes only through people, and their cooperation with one another. Time spent on the shop floor also helps to reduce functional barriers. But this principle of keeping in touch and exchanging ideas should not be limited to the workplace: it should extend to the suppliers, the customers and the distributors. If everyone is involved then *everyone* can contribute.

We believe that the role of the manager and supervisor can and should be quantified. A Japanese consultant, one Masaaki Imai, maintains that:

> Japanese management generally believes that a manager should spend at least 50 per cent of his time on improvement.

In view of this statement, it seems strange to us that management literature, especially that originating in the United States, maintains that the Americans are the innovators and the Japanese are mere copycats. We are sure that the reality is exactly the contrary. Whilst the United States may claim many a first, and a matchless stream of Nobel laureates, yet there the worker is still, for the most part, treated merely as a worker. Nothing more is asked of him, with the result that an enormous potential in terms of innovation remains untapped. It seems the same sort of thing happens with supervisors and middle managers. They are seen only as administrators: once again their ideas on the work they are doing are not sought. Innovation is not *expected* of them: the result – they are not creators of new ideas. They live up to expectation: they do what is required and expected of them and no more. On the other hand, Japan has created the proper climate for innovation, by insisting that everyone, right down to the worker on the shop floor, is involved in innovation. Their ideas are requested and acted upon. Further, the office personnel, suppliers, salesmen and sub-contractors are all treated as members of the larger team and asked to contribute their ideas. This cooperation has become all the more important with increasing computerisation and the interrelationship of all the operations.

VOLUME PRODUCTION NOT THE ANSWER

Through the sixties and seventies it was thought, particularly in the United States, that all the problems could be overcome by volume production. That would bring the profits. But that was a myth that has now been shattered. Those companies involved in renewal and regeneration of their activities have moved away from the volume growth concept. They look rather for increased quality and continuing innovation. The sacrifice of quality for the sake of volume, apart from being a sure recipe for economic disaster, also led to substantial worker unrest. Work lost its true meaning and the workers could no longer have pride in their work. General Electric's Dick Burke was very candid about the problem that faced the United States at this point. He said:

> The biggest problem in US industry today is the arrogance of management. We had nineteen thousand people here – a tremendous resource – but our management team hadn't communicated anything to them except, implicitly, the importance of volume . . . [on the basis] that hourly paid people aren't bright. Why should we take the trouble to instruct them or ask them for help?

Once again, management expected little from their workforce, and that is exactly what they got. As a result the situation at General Electric's Appliance Park works deteriorated to such an extent that work had lost its meaning even for middle managers. Absenteeism was at a very high level, time clocks were broken, the restrooms were a mess, and management had absolutely no backing.

It looked to be a losing situation, beyond redemption. Then Roger Schipke took charge, and the situation was transformed. Quality was made the prime cause and objective of the company, people were treated properly and every effort was made to demonstrate the principle 'we care'. Once the employees were convinced that management did indeed care, that there was every intention of doing something about the situation, they began to cooperate. They began to care as well. The emphasis on quality seems to be the key to caring.

This lesson now seems to have been learnt very well by the more progressive companies in the manufacturing sector, but it seems that most companies in the service sector have still to do so. If they fail to learn the lesson fast enough, they may well face the same disastrous situation as was faced by so many manufacturers some ten years ago. The secret to success in the service sector is disarmingly simple: offer good service! Quality is the key to it all.

When we assert that volume production is not the answer, and look around for illustrative case histories, one of our best sources of evidence must be industries with small-volume production. Typical of these is of course the high-quality sports car market. We have already discussed the example of Jaguar: Porsche offer us yet another example. There is no doubt that everyone likes to win, and the ability to win has a considerable influence on company morale. This is evidenced by the efforts that Jaguar have been making recently to win in the competitive races, such as the Le Mans Grand Prix, that are widely publicised. Coming back to Porsche, there was a time, the first time in its history, when the company was on the verge of making a loss. The management brought in Peter Schutz (of Cumins Engines) to take charge. His predecessor's strategy had been to shrink the business and hold on to a highly profitable niche in the market. But this had proved to be a losing strategy. In reply to the question asked by Schutz, when assessing the position: 'What is the all-time best car?' Professor Porsche, the visionary behind the Porsche car and also the designer of the world-famous VW Beetle, said: 'We haven't built it yet.' It was this attitude of mind that encouraged Schutz to follow his winning strategy.

When Schutz called a meeting of his managers, they all told him that there was no chance of their new turbo-engine car winning overall in the forthcoming Le Mans Grand Prix. He adjourned the meeting immediately, saying: 'So long as I am in charge of the company, we won't talk about not winning'. Then, at a meeting the following day, he set out a plan for winning. Everyone got excited, became committed to the cause, and rehearsed all the steps they would need to take to win. They only had 62 days to get ready, but they did it. They achieved what had been thought impossible and went on to win the race. Included in their team was an ace driver who had retired a couple of years earlier, but heard about their 'winning' model and offered to drive it. Thus there was total commitment to a cause and success was the result.

It seems that the key to success is to find a cause about which the employees can enthuse. Winning a race is one obvious one, but there are many others. Striving for quality seems to arouse a great deal of enthusiasm, together with causes such as cost reduction, and improved technology. There seems to be no limit to what can be achieved once the cause is there and has been successfully communicated to all the staff. There is no doubt that having a cause is a very powerful motivating factor, but to be meaningful it has to be translated into terms that all can understand. This is the challenge facing today's managers and leaders. For a cause to inspire people, so that they are committed, management needs to communicate that cause effectively. And let us not forget that a new cause is necessary when the present cause has served its purpose. We live in a fast-changing and dynamic world: people like change and something new. It becomes the task of managers to devise that for them.

References

CHAPTER 1

Adair J (a), *Developing Leaders – The Ten Key Principles*, McGraw Hill, 1988

Adair J (b), *Not Bosses but Leaders – How to Lead the Way to Success*, Kogan Page, 1988

Barrett F D, 'Teamwork – how to expand its power and punch', *Business Quarterly*, Winter 1987, pp 24–31

Bennis W and Nanus B, *Leaders – The Strategies for Taking Charge*, Harper & Row, USA, 1985

Blake R R, Mouton J S and Allen R L, *Spectacular Teamwork – How to Develop the Leadership Skills for Team Success*, John Wiley, USA, 1986

Cane A, 'The qualities a chief executive needs – leadership in the future', *Financial Times*, 7 September 1988

Carson I, 'Ahead of the field', *The Economist*, Vol 306, p 86

Fieldler F E and Chemers M M, *Improving Leadership Effectiveness – The Leader Match Concept*, (2nd ed), John Wiley, 1984

Fieldler F E and Garcia J E, *New Approaches to Effective Leadership – Cognitive Resources and Organisational Performance*, John Wiley, 1987

Golding C W, *What it Takes to Get to the Top – and Stay There*, Putman, USA, 1983

Jones J H, *Making it Happen – Reflections on Leadership*, Collins, 1988

News item: 'Teamwork lacking in cockpit', *Times of India*, 23 October 1988

Lorenz C, 'Scrum and Scramble' – The Japanese style, *Financial Times*, 19 June 1987, p 19

Maddux R B, *Team Building: An Exercise in Leadership*, Kogan Page, 1988

Maude B, *Leadership in Management*, Business Books, 1978

Pascale R T and Athos A G, *The Art of Japanese Management*, Sidgwick & Jackson, 1981

Purokayastha D, 'Teamwork responsible for current success', *Business India*, 23 Jan/5 Feb 1989, p 177

Reich R B, 'Entrepreneurship reconsidered – the team as a hero', *Harvard Business Review*, Vol 65, May–June 1987, pp 77–89

CHAPTER 2

Adair J, *Effective Teambuilding*, Gower, 1986

Argyle M, *The Social Psychology of Work*, Penguin, 1972

Ryan M, 'Teamwork in the City', *Journal of Management Development*, Vol 8, No 3, 1989, pp 14–20

Samuelson P A, 'A tribute to teamwork', *Journal of Institutional and Theoretical Economics*, Vol 143, No 2, pp 235–243

Simon B B and Farrell B A, *Training in Small Groups*, Pergamon, 1979

Vinten G, 'Education, training and action learning', *Internal Auditing*, Vol 12, September 1989, pp 3–7

CHAPTER 3

Kharbanda O P and Stallworthy E A, *Company Rescue*, Heinemann, 1987

Waterman R H Jr, *The Renewal Factor: How the Best Get and Keep the Competitive Edge*, Bantam Books, 1987

CHAPTER 4

Carlzon J, *Moments of Truth*, Ballinger Publishing, USA, 1987

Kanter R M, *The Change Masters – Innovation for Productivity in the American Corporation*, Simon & Schuster, 1983

Naisbitt J, *Megatrends: Ten New Directions Transforming our Lives*, Warner, 1982

Peters T and Austin N, *A Passion for Excellence – The Leadership Difference*, Collins, 1985

Peters T, *Thriving on Chaos – Handbook for a Management Revolution*, Tata McGraw-Hill (India), 1989

Sapre S A, *Abraham Maslow – Management Theory Z*, Directorate of Printing & Stationery, Bombay, India, 1976

Sapre S A, *Management Philosophers and Practitioners*, Directorate of Government Printing & Stationery, Maharashtra State, Bombay, India, 1980

Trevor M, *The Japanese Management Development System*, Frances Pinter, USA, 1986

CHAPTER 5

Harding H, *Management Appreciation – A Handbook for Personal Assistants and Administrators*, Pitman, 1987

Hayakawa S I, *Language in Thought and Action*, (4th ed), Harcourt Brace Jovanovich, 1978

Merrell V D, *Huddling – the Informal Way to Management Success*, American Management Association, 1979

Naisbitt J, *Megatrends: Ten New Directions Transforming our Lives*, Warner, 1982

Peters T and Austin N, *A Passion for Excellence: The Leadership Difference*, Collins, 1985

Pinchot, Gifford III, *Intrapreneuring: Why you Don't Have to Leave a Corporation to Become an Intrapreneur*, Harper & Row, New York, 1985

Waterman R H Jr, *The Renewal Factor: How the Best Get and Keep the Competitive Edge*, Bantam Books, 1987

Woodstock M, *Team Development Manual*, Gower, 1989

CHAPTER 6

Fisher D J, Rules of thumb for physical scientists, *Transactions Technical Publications*, 1988

Galbraith J R, *Organisation Design*, Addison Wesley, 1977

CHAPTER 7

Adair J, *Effective Teambuilding*, Gower, 1986

Bennett D, *Successful Team Building Through TA*, Amacom, New York, 1988

Cleland D I and King W R (eds), *Project Management Handbook*. See Chapter 30, 'Project Teams and the Human Group' by R E Hill and T L Somers, Van Nostrand, New York, 1985

Francis D and Young D, *Top Team Building*, Gower, 1989

Lock D (ed), *Project Management Handbook*. Chapter 24, 'Motivating the participants', F L Harrison, Gower, 1987

Maddux R B, *Team Building: An Exercise in Leadership*, Kogan Page, 1988

Peters T, *Thriving on Chaos: Handbook for a Management Revolution*, Tata McGraw-Hill (India), 1989. (Reprint of US 1987 ed)

Peters T and Austin N, *A Passion for Excellence: The Leadership Difference*, Collins, 1985

Platt S, Piepe R and Smyth J, *New Teams: A Game to Develop Group Skills*, Gower, 1988

Stallworthy E A and Kharbanda O P, *International Construction and the Role of Project Management*, Gower, 1985

Tarkenton F, *How to Motivate People*, Harper & Row, New York, 1986

Tse K K, *Marks & Spencer – Anatomy of Britain's Most Efficiently Managed Company*, Pergamon, 1985

Woodstock M, *Team Development Manual*, Gower, 1989

Woodstock M, *Activities for Team Building*, Gower, 1989

CHAPTER 8

Belbin R M, *Management Teams: Why They Succeed or Fail*, Heinemann, 1984

Bemelmans T M A, *Beyond Productivity: Information Systems Development for Organizational Effectiveness*, North-Holland, 1984

Garfield C, *Peak Performers – The New Heroes in Business*, Hutchinson, 1986

CHAPTER 9

Adair J, *The Action-Centred Leader: The Industrial Society*, Kogan Page, 1988

Cleland D I and King W R (eds), *Project Management Handbook*, 2nd ed. See Chapter 30, Project teams and the human group, by R E Hill and T L Somers, Van Nostrand, 1985

Hardaker M and Ward B K, 'Getting things done – how to make a team work', *Harvard Business Review*, November–December 1987, pp 112–117

Lawler E E III, *High Involvement Management: Participative Strategies for Improving Organisational Performance*, Jossey-Bass, USA, 1986

Waterman R H Jr, *The Renewal Factor: How the Best Get and Keep the Competitive Edge*, Bantam Books, 1987

CHAPTER 10

Abeggler J and Stalk G, *Kaisha – The Japanese Corporation*, Basic Books, USA, 1985

Peters T, *Thriving on Chaos: Handbook for a Management Revolution*, Tata McGraw-Hill (India), 1989

CHAPTER 11

Peters T and Austin N, *A Passion for Excellence: The Leadership Difference*, Collins, 1985

Stramy B *et al*, *Transforming the Workplace*, Princeton Research Press (USA), 1985

Thamhain H J and Wilemon D L, 'Building high performance engineering project teams', *IEEE Transactions Engineering Management*, Vol EM-34, No 3, August 1987, pp 130–137

Ulshak L, Nathanson L and Gillan P G, *Small Group Problem Solving – An Aid to Organisational Effectiveness*, Addison-Wesley (USA), 1981

Vogel E, *Japan as Number One – Lessons for America*, Cambridge University Press (USA), 1979

CHAPTER 12

Cohen S S, 'How to be a leader', *Readers Digest*, August 1989, pp 98–100

Kotter J P, *The Leadership Factor*, The Free Press (USA), 1988

Lock D (ed), *Project Management Handbook*, Gower, 1987

Maddux R B, *Team Building: An Exercise in Leadership*, Kogan Page, 1988

Peters T, *Thriving on Chaos: Handbook for a Management Revolution*, Tata McGraw-Hill (India), 1989. (Reprint of the 1987 US ed)

Toft L A, 'Project management – a personal view', *Proceedings of the Institute of Mechanical Engineers*, Vol 202, No B1, 1988, pp 19–27

Tse K K, *Marks & Spencer – Anatomy of Britain's Most Efficiently Managed Company*, Pergamon, 1985

Waterman R H Jr, *The Renewal Factor: How the Best Get and Keep the Competitive Edge*, Bantam Books, 1987

CHAPTER 13

Adair J, *The Action-Centred Leader*, Gower, 1986

Article, 'Bechtel's project managers', *Bechtel Briefs*, October 1979, pp 4–13 (published by Bechtel, San Francisco)

Main J, 'Wanted: leaders who can make a difference', *Fortune*, Vol 116, 28 September 1987, pp 72–7

McGinnis A L, *Bringing Out the Best in People*, Augsburg Publishing House (USA), 1985

Zanger J H, 'Leadership – Management's better half', *Training*, December 1985, p 48

CHAPTER 14

Baker R N, 'Success and failure patterns of projects in the least developed countries', paper presented at Internet's 7th World Congress on Project Management, Copenhagen, September 1982

Buchanan S, 'Returning from overseas can mean a backward step', *International Herald Tribune*, 30 October 1985

'Corporate Planning for an Uncertain Future', *Long Range Planning*, Vol 15, No 4, August 1982

Kamei M, 'Trustworthiness and foresight; requisites of good management', *JMA Newsletter*, 1 July 1986. (Translation of an article that appeared in *JMA Management News*, 10 May 1986)

Murray F T and Murray A H, 'Global managers for global business', *Sloan Management Review*, Winter 1986, pp 75–80

CHAPTER 15

Adair J, *Effective Teambuilding*, Gower, 1986

Harris M, 'IBM – more worlds to conquer', *Business Week*, 18 February 1985, pp 84–7

Kharbanda O P and Stallworthy E A, *Company Rescue: How to Manage a Business Turnaround*, Heinemann, 1987

Peters T, *Thriving on Chaos: Handbook for a Management Revolution*, Tata McGraw-Hill (India), 1989. (Reprint of the 1987 US ed)

Peters T and Austin N, *A Passion for Excellence: the Leadership Difference*, Collins, 1985

Peters T J and Waterman R H, *In Search of Excellence – Lessons from America's Best-Run Companies*, Sidgwick & Jackson, 1984

CHAPTER 16

Adair J, *Effective Teambuilding*, Gower, 1986

Jones H, *Making it Happen – Reflections on Leadership*, Collins, 1987

CHAPTER 17

Article: 'Kudremukh – looking ahead', *Business India*, 19 November/2 December 1984, p 117

Babani A, 'Robots – Malthusian explosion', *Herald Review*, 14 July 1985, pp 42–43

Belbin R M, *Management Teams: Why They Succeed or Fail*, Heinemann, 1984

Byrne J A, 'Whose robots are winning?', *Forbes*, Vol 131, 14 March 1983, p 154

Humphreys B, 'Working robots: have they arrived?', *Cost Engineering* (USA), Vol 27, No 1, January 1985, pp 50–57

Maude B, *Leadership in Management*, Business Books, 1978

Mirchandani H V, Kudremukh – inception and implementation, a section in 'Project management in public enterprises', published by the *Standing Conference of Public Enterprises*, New Delhi, part of the proceedings of a National Workshop organised jointly by SCOPE and the Bureau of Public Enterprises. See pages 4.6.1 to 4.6.22 and 9 annexes, 1983

Peters T and Austin N, *A Passion for Excellence: The Leadership Difference*, Collins, 1985

Pintz W S, *Ok Tedi – Evolution of a Third World Mining Project*, Mining Journal Books, 1984

CHAPTER 18

Crosby P B, *Quality Without Tears – The Art of Hassle-free Management*, McGraw-Hill, USA, 1985

Feigenbaum A V, 'ROI – How long before quality improvement pays off?', *Quality Program*, February 1987, pp 15–20

Irving R R, 'Weld quality: whose job is it?', *Iron Age*, 4 April 1986, p 67 + (5 pages)

Ishikawa K, *What is Total Quality Control – The Japanese Way*, Prentice Hall, 1985 (translated by David J Lu)

Nemoto M, *Total Quality Control for Management – Strategies and Techniques from Toyota and Toyoda Gosei*, Prentice Hall, USA, 1987 (translation from the Japanese by David J Lu)

Tallon R, 'How long before quality improvement pays off?', *Quality Progress*, February 1987, pp 19–20

Vaughn D, 'Quality management', *For Your Information*, M W Kellogg newsletter, May/June 1988, p 3

CHAPTER 19

Allen T, Katz R, Grady J J and Slavin N, Project team ageing and performance – the roles of projects and functional managers, *R&D Management*, Vol 18, No 4, 1988, pp 295–308

Harrington H J, 'Excellence – the IBM way', *IBM Technical Report*, 1986

Hull F, Azumi K and Wharton R, 'Suggestion rates and sociotechnical systems in Japanese *versus* American factories: beyond quality circles', *IEEE Transactions on Engineering Management*, Vol 35, No 1, February 1988, pp 11–24

Peters T and Austin N, *A Passion for Excellence: The Leadership Difference*, Collins, 1985

Peters T, *Thriving on Chaos: Handbook for a Management Revolution*, Tata McGraw-Hill (India), 1989. (Reprint of the 1987 US ed)

CHAPTER 20

Gully B A, Touran A and Asai T, 'Quality control circles in construction', *Journal of Construction Engineering*, Vol 113, No 3, September 1987, pp 427–439

Hansen B L and Ghare P M, *Quality Control and Application*, Prentice Hall, 1987

Hansen B L, *Quality Control: Theory and Applications*, Prentice Hall, 1963

Hutchins D, *Quality Circles Handbook*, Pitman, 1985

Ingle S, *Quality Circles Master Guide*, Prentice Hall, India, 1985

Ishikawa K, *What is Total Quality Control – The Japanese Way*, Prentice Hall, 1985 (translated by David J Lu)

Juran J M, *Quality Control Handbook*, McGraw Hill, New York, 3rd ed, 1974

Naisbitt J, *Megatrends: Ten New Directions Transforming our Lives*, Warner, 1982

Pall G A, *Quality Process Management*, Prentice Hall, 1987

Robson M, *Quality Circles – A Practical Guide*, Gower, 1982

Shetty Y K and Buehler V M, *Quality, Production and Innovation*, Elsevier, 1987

CHAPTER 21

Azumi K, Creativity of Japanese companies, *Japanese Foundation Newsletter*, Vol 14, No 4, December 1986, pp 12–15

Appendix

A Typical Position Description

Department   :   Project Team

Position   :   Manager, Project Cost Control

Reports to   :   Project Manager

Responsibilities: Establish, build up, maintain and improve a system for project cost control and the related estimating and reporting activities appropriate to the proposed project, in accordance with the principles set out in the 'Cost and Progress Control Manual' and the related 'Material Management Manual', together with the relevant sections of the project specification.

This will include, inter alia:

1   (a) Institute and maintain the appropriate administrative procedures in order to enable the above responsibility to be properly discharged.

    (b) Ensure the systematic development of site current estimates and cost control reports.

2   Receive commitment data from various sources, and data on the progress of work in the field from the various main and/or subcontractors for further progressing, including analysis and the preparation of the relevant reports.

3   Establish and maintain a system of monetary control on all bulk materials ordered, which can be related to the physical disposition of those materials.

4   Establish and maintain specific cost control activities in relation to open contracts (for example, cost plus or schedule of rates contracts), giving advice on the validity of invoices received, and appraisal of the efficiency or otherwise of such contracts, using the appropriate norms.

5   Establish and maintain a system of cost control, involving the comparison of actual with forecast progress in terms of both money and erection manhours, in order to discern trends, and report on exceptions, for others to take action as may be appropriate.

6   Provide forecasts, based on site current estimates, of the cash flow for the various separate projects constituting the investment.

7   Provide a service in relation to spot checks on the site activities, to enable reports to be issued on the effectiveness of the utilisation of labour, on the validity of work in progress appraisals made by the main contractors for the payment of subcontractors.

8   Contribute to the negotiation of contracts and variations to contracts for site work, estimating and agreeing where appropriate the value of such contracts, prior to approval by the Project Manager.

9   Coordinate with other departments both within the Project Team and at Head Office, to ensure that the projects are executed efficiently.

10 Coordinate with the Engineering and Finance Departments of the Owner to ensure that project cost control procedures are harmonised, and that there is a proper exchange of experience and data.

Index